THE STORY

of the

55th
(West Lancashire)
Division

By

THE REV. J. O. COOP, D.S.O., T.D., M.A.

Chaplain to the Forces First Class (T.F.)
Senior Chaplain of the Division

LIVERPOOL
"DAILY POST" PRINTERS
1919

IN proud memory of long days and nights in the trenches; of patrols, wiring parties and carrying parties; of supplies brought up and duty done by all ranks in all places; of many hours spent in digging; of days passed under shell fire, machine-gun fire and rifle fire; of raids by night and attacks by day; of a stubborn defence and a glorious advance, and the final overthrow of the enemy; of days, months and years devoted to the service of your KING and your COUNTRY.

In proud and solemn memory of the Fallen, and of all those who suffered wounds and mutilation in a just and righteous cause.

In proud hope of a glorious and lasting peace; of difficulties to be met and dangers overcome by cool heads and stout hearts; and of generations to come who shall prove themselves worthy of the great deeds of their Fathers.

(Lt.-Col. E. G. HOARE.)

CONTENTS.

	Page
Dedication	5
Preface	7
Foreword	8
Order of Battle	11
Chapter I. "Early Days"	19
Chapter II. "The Battle of the Somme"	30
Chapter III. "The Third Battle of Ypres"	46
Chapter IV. "The Battles of Cambrai"	65
Chapter V. "The Battle of Givenchy-Festubert"	85
Chapter VI. "The Advance"	124
Chapter VII. "The Last Phase"	160
Appendix I. Distinguishing Badges	165
Appendix II. Honours and Rewards	167
Appendix III. The First and Last Operation Orders	176
Appendix IV. Work of the R.E. and Pioneers	180
Appendix V. Battle Casualties	182

MAPS.

Battle of Guillemont	Aug. 8, 1916	Page 33
Battle of Ginchy	Sept. 9, 1916	38
Battle of Gueudecourt	Sept. 25, 1916	43
Battle of Ypres	July 31, 1917	51
Battle of Cambrai	Nov. 30, 1917	76
(The red line shews the Divisional Front at 7 a.m.)		
(The blue line shews the Divisional Front at 7 p.m.)		
Battle of Givenchy-Festubert—April 9, 1918—		
The Divisional Front at 4 a.m.		91
The Divisional Front at midnight		99
Map Shewing original Line (red) and the Line held (blue)		104
The Givenchy Craters	Aug. 24, 1918	126
Map Illustrating the Advance		Inset

PREFACE.

This history has been written primarily, not for the general public, but for the 57,000 Officers, Non-Commissioned Officers and men, still living, who made it; and for the relatives and friends of the glorious 6,000 whose mortal bodies rest in the soil of France and Flanders, but whose memory will never fade from the minds of their comrades-in-arms. If these find the book satisfactory, and if it in any small degree reminds them of the deeds which they and theirs accomplished, then I care not who else may find fault with it.

For the chapter on the capture of the craters, and the subsequent advance, I am greatly indebted to my friend, Lieut.-Colonel R. T. Lee, C.M.G., D.S.O., of the Divisional General Staff, who has very kindly given me permission to make use of his excellent and minute narrative.

J. O. COOP.

Headquarters, 55th Division.
    Brussels, March, 1919.

FOREWORD.

The compilation of the Story of the 55th Division was undertaken at my request by Colonel the Revd. J. O. Coop, D.S.O., who served as Senior Church of England Chaplain with the Division during the whole period to which the story relates. He has performed his task with the same zeal and care as he has shown in all other matters pertaining to the interests of the Division. He has asked me to write a foreword, but I feel that his work needs little introduction or explanation from me to recommend it to those who have served in the 55th Division or who are connected with it.

It is right that the deeds of the Division should live in story, not merely as a memorial of what the soldiers of all ranks who served in it accomplished, but as an example for all time of the spirit in which the dangers and hardships of the most frightful war in history were met by Englishmen; and as an inspiration for those who come after, and who, in their turn, may be called upon to play the game as it was played by those who went before them. It is impossible to describe the horrors of this war so as to bring even a faint image of them to the minds of those who have not actually witnessed them: it is equally impossible adequately to realize the courage, devotion to duty, determination, and endurance needed from the fighting men of the front line, who went through and surmounted them triumphantly and cheerily.

Major-General SIR HUGH SANDHAM JEUDWINE, K.C.B.

This present story can only give a bare outline, but fortunately it has been possible to preserve the records of numerous deeds of gallantry, and the personal narratives of many of the junior leaders who took part in assaults and hand to hand fighting. These records are at present in the custody of the 55th Division Comrades' Association. Some day it may be practicable to publish them. If so, it will help to a better understanding of what the junior Officers and the Rank and File of the Division have done to make its reputation.

No Story of the 55th Division could be complete without a tribute to our gallant comrades who have fallen under the Badge of the Rose. To the memory of these, and to the many others who have been permanently maimed while serving in its ranks, we, who have come unharmed through the campaign, owe the deepest reverence. Their sacrifices have not been in vain in the past. It is for us to ensure that they shall not prove so in the future.

H. S. JEUDWINE,
Major-General.
Commanding 55th (West Lancashire) Division.
(3rd January, 1916, to 15th March, 1919).

Bonn, 2nd June, 1919.

ORDER OF BATTLE.

Commander.	Major-General Sir H. S. JEUDWINE, K.C.B.
A.D.C. 1.	**Major M. H. Milner, D.S.O., M.V.O., Res. of Officers.**
A.D.C. 2.	Capt. E. A. W. Maude, North Irish Horse. **Capt. R. L. Dobell, 1/6th King's Liverpool Regt. (T.F.).**
G.S.O. 1.	Lt.-Col. J. K. Cochrane, Leinster Regt. (Brigadier-General, 1918). Lt.-Col. T. R. C. Price, C.M.G., D.S.O., Welsh Guards (Brig.-General, 1918). **Lt.-Col. R. T. Lee, C.M.G., D.S.O., Queen's (R.W. Surrey Regt.).**
G.S.O. 2.	Major J. G. Dill, D.S.O., Leinster Regt. (Brigadier-General, 1918). Lt.-Col. W. Wright, V.C. C.M.G., Queen's (R.W. Surrey Regt.). Major R. S. Popham, D.S.O., Notts and Derby Regt. Major V. A. Jackson, D.S.O., York and Lancaster Regt. Major Hon. E. C. Lascelles, D.S.O., M.C., Rifle Brigade. Major H. E. Pickering, M.C., West Yorkshire Regt. **Major M. J. A. Jourdier, D.S.O., East Surrey Regt.**
G.S.O. 3.	Capt. Hon. E. C. Lascelles, M.C., Rifle Brigade. Capt. J. N. Barstow, M.C., 4th W. Lanc. R.F.A. (T.F.). **Capt. G. Surtees, M.C., 8th Manchester Regt. (T.F.).**
A.A. & Q.M.G.	Lt.-Col. C. G. Liddell, D.S.O., Leicestershire Regt. **Lt.-Col. S. H. Eden, C.M.G., D.S.O., Black Watch.**

D.A.A.G.	Major G. N. Macready, D.S.O., M.C., R.E. (Lt.-Col., 1917). **Major R. P. Power, O.B.E., Royal Irish Fusiliers.**
D.A.Q.M.G.	Major Sir E. H. Preston, Bt., D.S.O., M.C., Royal Sussex Regt. (Lt., Col., 1918). **Major H. R. Kerr, M.C., Royal Army Service Corps.**
A.D.M.S.	Col. J. J. Russell, C.B., A.M.S. (Major-General, 1918). Col. R. Jackson, T.D., A.M.S. Col. B. Watts, D.S.O., A.M.S. Col. H. D. Brook, V.D., A.M.S. Col. H. S. Thurston, C.B., C.M.G., A.M.S. **Col. H. G. Martin, C.M.G., A.M.S.**
D.A.D.M.S.	Lt.-Col. B. Watts, R.A.M.C. Major S. D. Large, D.S.O., M.C., R.A.M.C. **Major J. W. G. H. Riddel, M.C., R.A.M.C. (T.F.).**
Senior Chaplain, C/E.	**Rev. J. O. Coop, D.S.O., T.D., C.F. 1st Class (T.F.).**
,, ,, Non C/E.	Rev. T. Browne, C.F. 3rd Class.
A.P.M.	Major J. D. Barry, 5th Lancers. Capt. R. A. L. Meynell, Shropshire L.I. **Capt. C. W. Trevelyan, M.C., London Rifle Brigade (T.F.).**
D.A.D.V.S.	**Major A. Spreull, D.S.O., A.V.S. (T.F.).**
D.A.D.O.S.	Capt. E. O. Collison. Capt. C. W. Arnett, M.C. Capt. E. G. Davies. **Major H. Jenken.**

Royal Artillery.

Commander.	Brig.-Gen. J. J. MacMahon, R.A. **Brig.-Gen. A. M. Perreau, C.B., C.M.G., R.A.**

13

Brigade Major.	Major R. Benson, D.S.O., R.A.
	Major R. B. Warton, D.S.O., R.A.
Staff Captain.	Major E. V. Hemelryk, D.S.O., 4th W. Lancs. R.F.A. (T.F.)
	Capt. D. M. Ritchie, M.C., 1st W. Lancs. R.F.A. (T.F.).
275 Brigade, R.F.A.	Lt.-Col. L. J. Osborn, D.S.O., V.D.
	Lt.-Col. H. C. Sheppard, C.M.G., D.S.O. (Brigadier-General, 1916).
	Lt.-Col. E. B. Cotter, D.S.O.
	Lt.-Col. W. J. K. Rettie, D.S.O.
	Lt.-Col. C. E. Walker, D.S.O., T.D., C.M.G.
276 Brigade, R.F.A.	Lt.-Col. T. E. Topping, C.B., C.M.G., D.S.O., T.D. (Brig.-General, 1918).
	Lt.-Col. R. Stead, T.D.
	Lt.-Col. E. W. Grove, D.S.O.
	Lt.-Col. D. Pudsey, D.S.O.
277 Brigade, R.F.A.	Lt.-Col. J. P. Reynolds, D.S.O., T.D.
(Army Troops, 1917)	Lt.-Col. J. E. C. J. Cochrane, D.S.O.
55th Div. Ammn. Col.	Lt.-Col. A. R. Braid.
	Col. E. A. Lambart, C.B.
D.T.M.O.	Capt. V. E. Cotton, 4th W. Lancs., R.F.A.
	Capt. K. V. Wright, M.C.

Royal Engineers.

Commander.	Lt.-Col. J. E. E. Craster, R.E.
	Lt.-Col. C. B. Bonham, D.S.O., R.E.
	Lt.-Col. O. C. Brandon, C.M.G., D.S.O.
Adjutant.	Capt. G. D. De'Ath, M.C., R.E.
	Capt. R. Carr, M.C., R.E. (T.F.).
	Capt. G. S. Hallas, M.C., R.E., (T.F.).
	Capt. J. H. Forshaw, M.C., R.E. (T.F.).
419 Field Co., R.E.	Major H. L. Campbell, D.S.O., T.D. (Lt.-Col., 1916).
	Major A. D. Murray.
	Major A. Russell, D.S.O.
422 Field Co., R.E.	Major C. T. Brown, D.S.O., T.D.
	Major H. C. Fry, M.C.

423 Field Co., R.E.   Major E. Matthews, M.C.
                       Major T. R. McMahon.
                       Major R. H. Warde, M.C.
55th Divl. Signal Co. Major W. Oppenheim, M.C.
                       Major C. E. Tebbitt, M.C.
                       Major A. G. Richardson, M.C.

R.A.M.C.

1/3rd W. Lancs.   Lt.-Col. A. G. Gullan.
   Field Ambulance.   **Lt.-Col. R. Coffey, D.S.O.**
2/1st W. Lancs.
   Field Ambulance.   **Lt.-Col. J. Wood, D.S.O.**
2/1st Wessex   Lt. Col. A. F. W. Sayres. (Killed 1917.)
   Field Ambulance.   **Lt.-Col. W. Blackwood, D.S.O.**

164th Infantry Brigade.

Commander.   Brig.-General G. T. G. Edwards, C.B.
                       Brig.-General C. I. Stockwell, C.B., C.M.G., D.S.O., Royal Welsh Fusiliers.
Brigade Major.   Capt. V. A. Jackson, D.S.O., York and Lancaster Regt.
                       Capt. C. E. Thompson, D.S.O., M.C., South Lancs. Regt.
                       Capt. C. L. Chute, M.C., General List.
Staff Captain.   Capt. J. Fisher, K.O. Royal Lancaster Regt. (T.F.).
                       Capt. G. H. Teall, Lincolnshire Regt.
                       Capt. A. Warburton, D.S.O., M.C., 1/6th King's (Liverpool Regt.)
1/4th King's Own (Royal Lancaster Regt.)
                       Lt.-Col. F. M. Carleton, D.S.O. (Brig.-General, 1916.)
                       Lt.-Col. J. L. Swainson. (Killed, 1916.)
                       Lt.-Col. G. B. Balfour, D.S.O.
                       Lt.-Col. R. Gardner, M.C.
1/8th King's (L'pool Regt.). Transferred to 57th Div., 1918.
                       Lt.-Col. E. A. Fagan, D.S.O. (Brig.-General, 1916.)
                       Major H. Leech. (Killed 1917.)
                       Lt.-Col. G. C. Heath, D.S.O.

2/5th Lancashire Fusiliers.
Lt.-Col. H. J. Shirley.
Lt.-Col. R. W. Fox.
Lt.-Col. C. J. B. Bridgwater.
Lt.-Col. B. Best-Dunkley, V.C. (Killed 1917.)
Lt.-Col. G. S. Brighten, D.S.O.

1/4th Loyal North Lancashire Regt.
Lt.-Col. R. Hindle, D.S.O. (Killed 1917.)
Lt.-Col. J. A. Crump, D.S.O.
Lt.-Col. T. G. Williams, D.S.O., M.C.

165th Infantry Brigade.

Commander.
Brig.-General F. J. Duncan, C.M.G., D.S.O., Royal Scots. (Major-General, 1918.)
Brig.-General L. B. Boyd-Moss, C.M.G., D.S.O., South Staffordshire Regt.

Brigade Major.
Major G. H. Barnett, K.R. Rifle Corps.
Capt. W. Newton. (Killed 1916.)
Capt. A. H. K. Jackson, D.S.O., M.C., R. Warwickshire Regt.
Major Sir E. F. D. Pauncefort-Duncombe, Bart., D.S.O., Bucks Hussars.
Capt. C. Adderley-Taylor, M.C., 1/5th King's (Liverpool Regt.).

Staff Captain.
Capt. A. G. Cousins, 24th London Regt.
Capt. A. H. K. Jackson, R. Warwickshire Regt.
Capt. J. H. T. Priestman, Lincolnshire Regt.
Major J. G. Thompson, D.S.O., M.C., 1/7th King's (Liverpool Regt.)

1/5th King's (Liverpool Regt.).
Lt.-Col. J. J. Shute, D.S.O., T.D.
Lt.-Col. A. Buckley, D.S.O.
Lt.-Col. J. J. Shute, C.M.G., D.S.O., T.D.

1/6th King's (Liverpool Regt.).
Lt.-Col. E. J. Harrison.
Lt.-Col. R. Wainwright, T.D.
Lt.-Col. J. B. McKaig, D.S.O.

1/7th King's (Liverpool Regt.)
        Lt.-Col. S. C. Marriott.
        Lt.-Col. C. K. Potter, D.S.O., M.C.
1/9th King's (L'pool Regt.). Transferred to 57th Div., 1918.
        Lt.-Col. F. W. Ramsay, C.M.G., D.S.O.
        (Major-General, 1918.)
        Lt.-Col. C. G. Bradley.
        Major H. K. S. Woodhouse, D.S.O.
        Lt.-Col. F. W. M. Drew, D.S.O.

166th Infantry Brigade.

Commander.   Brig.-General L. F. Green-Wilkinson, D.S.O., Rifle Brigade.
        Brig.-General F. G. Lewis, C.B., C.M.G., T.D., Kensington Rifles.
        Brig.-General R. J. Kentish, C.M.G., D.S.O., Royal Irish Fusiliers.

Brigade Major.   Major J. M. Hamilton, D.S.O., Gordon Highlanders.
        Capt. B. B. von B. Im Thurn, M.C., Hampshire Regt.
        Capt. A. R. Abercrombie, M.C., Queen's Royal West Surrey Regt.
        Capt. H. Carter, M.C., London Rifle Brigade (T.F.).

Staff Captain.   Lieut. Stopford.
        Capt. E. H. D. Stocker, M.C., 1/9th King's (Liverpool Regt.)
        Capt. H. R. Kerr, M.C., Army Service Corps.
        Capt. H. W. Jones, M.C.

1/5th King's Own (Royal Lancaster Regt.).
        Lt.-Col. F. Eaves, D.S.O.
        Lt.-Col. C. A. W. Anderson. (Killed, 1916.)
        Lt.-Col. R. H. Anderson-Morshead. (Killed, 1918.)
        Lt.-Col. A. B. Wayte, D.S.O.
        Lt.-Col. E. G. Hoare, D.S.O.

1/10th Liverpool Scottish.
        Lt.-Col. J. R. Davidson, C.M.G.
        Lt.-Col. F. W. M. Drew, D.S.O.
        Lt.-Col. J. L. A. Macdonald, D.S.O.
        Lt.-Col. D. C. D. Munro, D.S.O., M.C., D.C.M.

1/5th South Lancashire Regt.
        Lt-Col. L. E. Pilkington, C.M.G.
        Lt.-Col. C. P. James, D.S.O.
        Lt.-Col. McCarthy-O'Leary.
        Lt. Col. C. E. Thompson, D.S.O., M.C.

1/5th Loyal North Lanc. Regt. Transferred to 57th Div., 1918.
        Lt.-Col. G. Hesketh, D.S.O., T.D.
        Lt.-Col. G. D. Morton, M.C.

Pioneer Battalion, 1/4th South Lancashire Regt.
        Lt.-Col. B. Fairclough, C.M.G., D.S.O.
        Lt.-Col. E. Fairclough. (Killed, 1918.)
        Lt.-Col. T. Ridgway, D.S.O., M.C.

Headquarters Divl. Train.
        Lt.-Col. A. R. Liddell, D.S.O.
        Lt.-Col. H. W. J. Carey.
        Lt.-Col. C. D. E. Upton.
        Lt.-Col. C. G. Allen, M.C.

55th Bn. Machine Gun Corps.
        Lt.-Col. H. W. Bolton, D.S.O.

The names in thicker type indicate the holder of the office at the conclusion of hostilities.

GLOSSARY.

G.S.O. .... General Staff Officer.
A.A. & Q.M.G. ..... Asst. Adjutant and Quartermaster General.
D.A.A.G. .... Deputy Asst. Adjutant General.
D.A.Q.M.G. .... Deputy Asst. Quartermaster General.
A.D.M.S. .... Asst. Director of Medical Services.
A.P.M. .... Asst. Provost Marshal.
D.A.D.V.S. .... Deputy Asst. Director of Veterinary Services.
D.A.D.O.S. .... Deputy Asst. Director of Ordnance Stores.
D.T.M.O. .... Divisional Trench Mortar Officer.

CHAPTER I.

EARLY DAYS.

The Act of Parliament authorising the creation of the Territorial Force became law in April, 1908, and the existing Artillery Brigades, Engineer Companies, and Infantry Battalions of the old Volunteer Force, together with the Imperial Yeomanry Cavalry of West Lancashire, immediately became the nucleus of the West Lancashire Division, T.F. Army Service Corps Companies, Signal Companies, Field Ambulances, and all other component parts of a Division were energetically recruited in the area extending Northwards from the Mersey to the Lune, and within a few months the Division had ceased to be a unit on paper: it existed.

It was very soon after the passing of the Act creating the Territorial Force that Lord Derby, who had been appointed President of the Territorial Association of West Lancashire, announced publicly that although, personally, he was strongly in favour of a measure of Universal compulsory service, he was nevertheless anxious to give Lord Haldane's scheme the fairest possible trial, and to that end he intended to spare no efforts to make the newly created West Lancashire Division the most efficient Territorial Division in the country. His manifest enthusiasm immediately secured the co-operation of all commanding officers and heads of public bodies in West Lancashire, and so zealously was the scheme taken in hand, that in August, 1909—after inspection by His Majesty King Edward VII. at Knowsley a month previously—the Division as a complete unit was able to proceed to Caerwys in North Wales for its first annual training. It was the first complete Territorial Division to take the field.

At Caerwys the Division received a visit from the French General Langlois, who thoroughly inspected it. General Langlois had been despatched by the French Government to report upon the possibilities of the Territorial Force, and he witnessed several operations of the Division in the Field, paid particular attention to the work of the Field Artillery, and his kindly but candid criticisms—subsequently published—were appreciated and seriously taken to heart. All ranks strove to bring the Division up to the high standard required by Lord Derby, and in the years which followed, under Major-General E. C. Bethune, its first commander, and subsequently under Major-General Walter Lindsay, such progress was made that upon the outbreak of war in August, 1914, the West Lancashire Division was at least the equal of any Territorial Division in the country.

The Division had just begun its annual training when war was declared. Its composition at that time was as follows :—

The Lancashire Hussars.	Divisional Cavalry.
1st West Lancs. Brigade R.F.A.	Liverpool.
2nd West Lancs. Brigade R.F.A.	Preston.
3rd West Lancs. Brigade R.F.A.	Liverpool.
4th West Lancs. (Howr) Bde. R.F.A.	Liverpool.
West Lancs. Divl. Royal Engineers	St. Helens.

North Lancashire Infantry Brigade.

4th King's Own R. Lancaster Regt.	Barrow.
5th King's Own R. Lancaster Regt.	Lancaster.
4th Loyal North Lancs. Regt.	Preston.
5th Loyal North Lancs. Regt.	Bolton.

Liverpool Infantry Brigade.
    5th King's (Liverpool Regt.)   Liverpool.
    6th (Rifle) King's (Liverpool Regt.)   Liverpool.
    7th King's (Liverpool Regt.)   Liverpool.
    8th (Irish) King's (Liverpool Regt.)   Liverpool.

South Lancashire Infantry Brigade.
    9th King's (Liverpool Regt.)   Liverpool.
    10th (Scottish) King's (Liverpool Regt.) Liverpool.
    4th South Lancashire Regt.   Warrington.
    5th South Lancashire Regt.   St. Helens.

West Lancashire Army Service Corps.

Royal Army Medical Corps.
    1st West Lancs. Field Ambulance.   Liverpool.
    2nd West Lancs. Field Ambulance.   Liverpool.
    3rd West Lancs. Field Ambulance.   St. Helens.

Hardly had the units reached the Training area when they were recalled to their Peace Stations and Mobilisation was commenced. Those early days will be vividly remembered by all who had part in them. The various barracks and depots were besieged by crowds of first-rate recruits; every existing vacancy was filled and could have been filled ten times over. Within a few hours of the Order for Mobilisation the War strength personnel of the Division was complete. A day or two later came the telegram from Lord Kitchener inviting units to volunteer for service overseas. The response was immediate and emphatic. Every unit in the Division volunteered.

General Lindsay left the Division to join Sir John French's Staff a few days after mobilisation. He was succeeded by Major-General Hammersley who, also, after a brief period of command, proceeded overseas, and the Division was ordered to Kent for training under the command of Major-General J. B. Forster. The necessities of the military situation in Flanders, however, prevented the Division from going out as a complete unit as had been intended. Reinforcements were urgently required for the Regular Army, and so from October, 1914, to May, 1915, a steady flow of battalions, R.E. companies, and Field Ambulances from the Division proceeded overseas where they were attached to units of the Regular Army and served with them during the operations of 1915. The Liverpool Scottish embarked for France at the end of October, 1914—and the remaining Infantry battalions, in quick succession, in the early months of 1915. The North Lancashire Brigade, re-composed, was attached to the 51st (Highland) Division and served with them until the West Lancashire Division was re-formed in January, 1916. The Artillery of the Division were retained for service in England until September, 1915, when they embarked with the 2nd Canadian Division and served with them until the middle of December.

It was about this time that rumour began to spread that the long-desired hope was to be realised and that the Division was at last to have the opportunity, which its preparedness at the outbreak of war had denied to it, of fighting as a complete unit. It cannot be denied that there was some little heart-burning, both at home and overseas, that the Division should have been split up ; and, though proud of the fact that the various units should have been regarded sufficiently efficient to be drafted overseas and merged into Regular Divisions, there was a deep desire that the old Division should have an opportunity of making a name for itself as a

Division. When, therefore, the Artillery suddenly received orders to proceed to the neighbourhood of St. Omer in mid-December, 1915—and when it became known that other units of the Division had received orders to leave the Divisions to which they had been attached, and to proceed to the back areas—rumour became persistent, and subsequently proved to be true, that all the units of the old Division were to be re-concentrated, and that the Division would, henceforward, fight as the 55th (West Lancashire) Division.

It was, therefore, a Division composed of units which had had some war experience, which began to assemble in and around Hallencourt, near Abbeville, on and after January 3rd, 1916. In the battles of Hill 60, St. Eloi, 2nd battle of Ypres, Hooge, Festubert and Loos, its battalions and companies had played their part and had given full evidence of their capabilities. The general morale and esprit de corps were alike excellent and it was plainly evident that, congregated in those small French villages around Hallencourt was the material of a first rate fighting force. The composition of the Division was as under:—

"A" Squadron North Irish Horse.
1st West Lancs. Cyclist Company.

Divisional Artillery.
1st West Lancs. Brigade R.F.A.
2nd West Lancs. Brigade R.F.A.
3rd West Lancs. Brigade R.F.A.
4th West Lancs. (How.) Brigade. R.F.A.
Divisional Ammunition Column.

Divisional Engineers.
1/1st West Lancs. Field Coy. R.E.

2/1st West Lancs. Field Coy. R.E.
2/2nd West Lancs. Field Coy. R.E.
Divisional Signal Company.

164*th Infantry Brigade.*
    1/4th King's Own Royal Lancaster Regt.
    1/8th (Irish) King's (Liverpool Regt.)
    2/5th Lancashire Fusiliers.
    1/4th Loyal North Lancashire Regt.

165*th Infantry Brigade.*
    1/5th King's (Liverpool Regt.)
    1/6th King's (Liverpool Regt.)
    1/7th King's (Liverpool Regt.)
    1/9th King's (Liverpool Regt.)

166*th Infantry Brigade.*
    1/5th King's Own Royal Lancaster Regt.
    1/10th (Scottish) King's (Liverpool Regt.)
    1/5th South Lancashire Regt.
    1/5th Loyal North Lancs. Regt.

Pioneer Battalion.
    1/4th South Lancashire Regt.

Divisional Train.

Royal Army Medical Corps.
    1/3rd West Lancs. Field Ambulance.
    2/1st West Lancs. Field Ambulance.
    2/1st Wessex Field Ambulance.

Sanitary Section.

1*st West Lancs. Mobile Veterinary Section.*

To the command of the Division was appointed Major-General H. S. Jeudwine, C.B., and to him it was given to mould the pliable material ready to hand. The subsequent history of the Division is evidence sufficient of the extent to which he succeeded. No General ever

Brussels, 3/1/19

Major R. P. Power, o.b.e.   Major M. J. A. Jourdier, d.s.o.

Capt. G. Surtees, m.c.   Lt.-Col. R. T. Lee, c.m.g., d.s.o.   Major M. H. Milner, d.s.o., m.v.o.   Capt. Noble, m.c.

Lt.-Col. S. H. Eden, c.m.g., d.s.o.   The Earl of Derby, k.g.   Major-General Sir H. S. Jeudwine, k.c.b.   The Earl of Athlone, g.c.b.

was more devoted to his Division: no Division ever was more devoted to its General.

On January 29th, 1916, the Division paraded as a complete unit, for the first time since the outbreak of war, for inspection by Lieut. General the Earl of Cavan, Commanding XIV Corps, and a few days later proceeded to relieve the 88th French Division—at that time occupying the sector South of Arras from Wailly to Bretencourt. The relief was completed by the 16th February, and the Division immediately began to make its presence felt. To harass the enemy as much as possible ; to keep him ever upon the alert ; to lose no opportunity of inflicting casualties upon him—these were from the first the methods drilled into the Division, and the enemy was not slow in learning to appreciate them.

The period from February 16th to the end of July, when the Division left the Gouy area to take part in the battle of the Somme, was a period of trench warfare, with raids of recurring frequency and recurring strength. To mention these raids in any detail would be impossible here : two of them, however, call for more than a passing notice.

It was on the night of the 17th April that the first raid on a large scale was attempted by the Division. Specially trained volunteers from the Liverpool Irish were selected to carry out the raid, and all details were carefully worked out and practised beforehand. The plan adopted, and subsequently successfully carried out, was to await propitious weather conditions, to cut the wire beforehand by hand and then, when the raiding parties were entering the enemy trenches, to put down a heavy box barrage round the spot to be raided. The weather conditions on the night of the 16th April proved to be suitable, and at midnight the wire-cutting party went out. They were, however, delayed—in the first place by an enemy working party, and in the second place by the fact that the wire proved to be a good deal thicker than was contemplated, and cutting was the more difficult. As a result it was impossible to complete the work before dawn, so the raid was postponed. The following evening, however, proved equally propitious. After a spell of bright moonlight the sky clouded over, and, as the enemy had apparently not noticed that his wire had been cut the night before, it was decided that the raid should be carried out.

First of all the wire-cutting party went out to make certain that the work had been completed, and a heavy machine gun barrage was put down to drown the sound of the wire-cutters. Then at a given signal the Artillery opened fire and the storming party entered the enemy trenches. The party was divided into two sections, each led by an officer, to work to the right and left of the trench. A sentry was promptly shot by the officer leading the left party, all telephone wires were pulled down and cut, and both parties proceeded to work right and left along the trench. All the enemy seen were killed; three dug-outs were bombed, and a grenade store was blown up. The whole of the party returned safely to our lines except the officer commanding the left party, who, in performing a very gallant action, for which he was posthumously awarded the Victoria Cross, sacrificed his life. (The details of this action will be found in the Appendix). From prisoners captured subsequently it was ascertained that no fewer than 56 of the enemy had been accounted for, either by the raiding party or by the Artillery barrage. The prisoners stated also that very considerable damage had been done to their dug-outs and trenches. Altogether the raid had proved a cleverly conceived, admirably executed, and wonderfully successful piece of work.

On June 28th a daylight raid on a pretentious scale took place. Again the preparations were careful and detailed; gas and smoke were to be discharged on a two mile front, to be followed by raids in no fewer than six different places by parties from the 2/5th Lancashire Fusiliers, 1/4th Loyal North Lancs., and the 1/5th, 1/6th, 1/7th and 1/9th Liverpools. Unfortunately at the crucial moment a change of wind took place and the discharge of gas was only partially successful. In addition the raiding parties were received with heavy rifle and machine gun fire, with the result that two of the parties were unable to penetrate the enemy trenches. The remainder, however, were successful, and many of the enemy were killed. The following day the subjoined Special Order of the Day was issued by the Major General Commanding :—

" 29th June, 1916.

" Yesterday six raids on the enemy's trenches were carried out by the 2/5th Lancashire Fusiliers and 1/4th Loyal North Lancashire Regiment, of the 164th Infantry Brigade, and by the 1/5th, 1/6th, 1/7th and 1/9th King's Liverpool Regiments, of the 165th Infantry Brigade, assisted by detachments of the Royal Engineers. These raids were carried out in daylight in unaccustomed and very difficult circumstances, and in the face of very determined opposition. In spite of these obstacles the results aimed at were successfully obtained, and great damage and loss inflicted on the enemy. The gallantry, devotion, and resolution shown by all ranks was beyond praise, and the Major-General Commanding is proud to be able to congratulate the West Lancashire Division on the discipline and soldierly spirit exhibited—a discipline and spirit which the most seasoned troops could not have surpassed.

"He wishes also to congratulate the Artillery, and all the Medium and Light Trench Mortar Batteries engaged, on the very determined and efficient support which they gave to the enterprise, in some cases under circumstances of considerable danger.

"He deeply regrets the loss of those who fell, but the spirit they showed will have its effect on the enemy. When the opportunity comes of avenging their deaths the Major-General Commanding is confident that the Division will not forget them."

It was in the month of May, during our occupation of this sector of the line south of Arras, that an important change took place in the organisation of the Divisional Artillery. The Brigades were re-formed so as to consist each of three 18-pr. Batteries and one 4.5 in. Howitzer Battery. New names were given to them and the old names were lost except in the memory of those who had served in the Brigades in the years before the war. The old 1st, 2nd, 3rd and 8th Lancashire Batteries became A, B, C and D Batteries of the 275th Brigade; the 9th, 10th, 11th and 7th Lancashire Batteries became A, B, C and D Batteries of the 276th Brigade; and the 12th, 13th, 14th and R Battery of the 4th West Lancs. Brigade became A, B, C and D Batteries of the 277th Brigade. In addition the 1st, 2nd and 3rd West Lancashire Brigades each formed a new 18-pr. Battery, which became A, B and C Batteries of the 278th Brigade.

Thus the old 1st West Lancs. R.F.A. (plus one Battery of the 4th West Lancs.) henceforth was to be known as the 275th Brigade R.F.A. ; the 2nd West Lancs. R.F.A. (plus one Battery of the 4th West Lancs. R.F.A.) was to be known as the 276th Brigade R.F.A., and the 3rd West Lancs. R.F.A. (plus a Battery of the 4th West Lancs. R.F.A.) became the 277th Brigade R.F.A. The 278th was a composite Brigade drawn from the existing Brigades as has been stated. All ranks were sorry to lose the old Territorial designation, but it had been for some time previously recognised to be inevitable. In this month, also, the Squadron of North Irish Horse, together with the Divisional Cyclist Company, left the Division to become Corps Troops.

Nothing of further importance took place during our tenure of this front. It had been a period of steady and progressive training for the more serious days soon to come, and had been invaluable in that it had also permitted the organisation of the many details which make for the efficiency and comfort of a Division. That it was by no means a peaceful period is shown by the casualty list: 63 Officers and 1,047 other ranks killed, wounded or missing. The Division was finding itself.

CHAPTER II.

THE BATTLE OF THE SOMME.

It was on the 25th of July that the Division was relieved by the 11th Division and proceeded South to play its part in the battle of the Somme. It had already co-operated in the attack of the Fourth Army on July 1st, by carrying out an intense bombardment on the whole Divisional front. Not only were many casualties inflicted on the enemy, but this operation had the required effect of causing a diversion and of preventing the enemy from withdrawing guns from our front. The journey South was accomplished rapidly and without incident, and on July 30th the Division had taken its appointed place in the line opposite the village of Guillemont—already a storm centre—and presently to receive dread notoriety.

Guillemont had proved to be a thorn in the British side, and had held up more then one attack. Its capture was of supreme importance to the success of the general advance, and a further attack which was entrusted to the Division was presently to take place. The Division, therefore, took over the line opposite Guillemont, as has been stated, on July 30th, and the 164th Infantry Brigade together with a company of the 1/4th South Lancs. (Pioneers) and the 2/1st (now 422 Coy.) R.E., less 2 sections, occupied the front, having the 39th French Division on its right, and the 2nd Division on its left. As a matter of fact the 164th Infantry Brigade had been selected to carry out the projected attack on Guillemont, but it incurred such very heavy casualties during its occupation of the line preliminary to the attack, that it was decided to send up also the 165th Infantry Brigade, and this Brigade together with another company of the Pioneers and the 1/1st West Lancs. (now 419th) Field Coy R.E. took over a portion of the front on the right.

The attack of Guillemont was timed to take place at 4-20 on the morning of the 8th August. The Order of Battle was as follows:—the 165th Infantry Brigade on the right, employing the 1/5th Liverpools and two companies of the 1/6th Liverpools, was to capture the line, roughly the Hardecourt-Guillemont road, and to couple up with the French on their right. The 164th Infantry Brigade, on the left, employing the 1/4th King's Own Royal Lancasters and the 1/8th Liverpool Irish, with two companies of the 1/4th Loyal North Lancs., was to take the northern and southern portions of Guillemont village respectively—the two companies of the Loyal North Lancs. following up the attack and occupying the German front line. The Liverpool Irish were to establish touch with the 2nd Division on the left of Guillemont station. The Divisional Artillery, with the assistance of other artillery attached for the purpose, was to support the attack by a creeping barrage —a method of support at that time in its infancy—and during the whole of the day on the 7th and until zero hour on the 8th they, together with the Heavy Artillery, kept up a continuous bombardment of the enemy positions and particularly of Guillemont village, which was known to be a strongly fortified place, the south-east corner especially containing a network of deep galleries holding large numbers of Infantry and machine guns. This bombardment was almost awe-inspiring in its intensity, and it might have been, with good reason, thought that nothing could live through it.

THE BATTLE FOR GUILLEMONT.

The attack took place at 4-20 a.m., as arranged, and at 5-20 a.m. a report was received to the effect that British troops were in Guillemont Station. A little later it became known that the centre had been unable to advance and the artillery barrage had to be brought back. The 1/4th Royal Lancasters had found a belt of the enemy's wire about 200 yards from their jumping off place—probably put out by the enemy during the night. They made a gallant attempt to cut their way through, but suffered so heavily from rifle and machine gun fire both from their front and from their right flank, that they were compelled to return to their trenches.

The position of the 1/8th Liverpools (Irish), who were reported to have reached Guillemont Station, in consequence of this became precarious. Their right flank was in the air and they were being subjected to heavy machine gun fire from Guillemont. They, therefore, attempted to bomb downwards from the north, and, though it is not clear whether they succeeded by this means or by their initial attack, they nevertheless did reach and did hold the northern end of the village.

At 7-15 a.m. the 2/5th Lancashire Fusiliers, which formed the left Brigade reserve, had been absorbed into the fight, and suffered severely from the enemy's barrage and from machine gun fire. A battalion of the 166th Infantry Brigade was sent up to take their place as Brigade Reserve.

Meanwhile the attack on the right had succeeded. The 165th Infantry Brigade, after successfully overcoming

DIVISIONAL HEADQUARTERS STAFF, *Dec., 1916.*

Top row: Capt. E. H. Preston, Capt. R. A. L. Meynell, Lieut. A. Leger, Capt. S. D. Large, Capt. C. W. Arnett, Capt. E. A. W. Maude, Major R. S. Popham Count Depret, Major M. H. Milner, Capt. J. N. Barstow, Capt. G. N. Macready, Major A. Spreull.

Bottom row: Col. R. Jackson, Brig.-General A. M. Perreau, Lt.-Col. J. K. Cochrane, Major-General H. S. Jeudwine, Lt.-Col. C.G. Liddell, Col. Rev. J. O. Coop

difficulties, captured and consolidated its objective, and the extreme left company—" D " Company of the 1/5th Liverpools—even succeeded in laying and maintaining

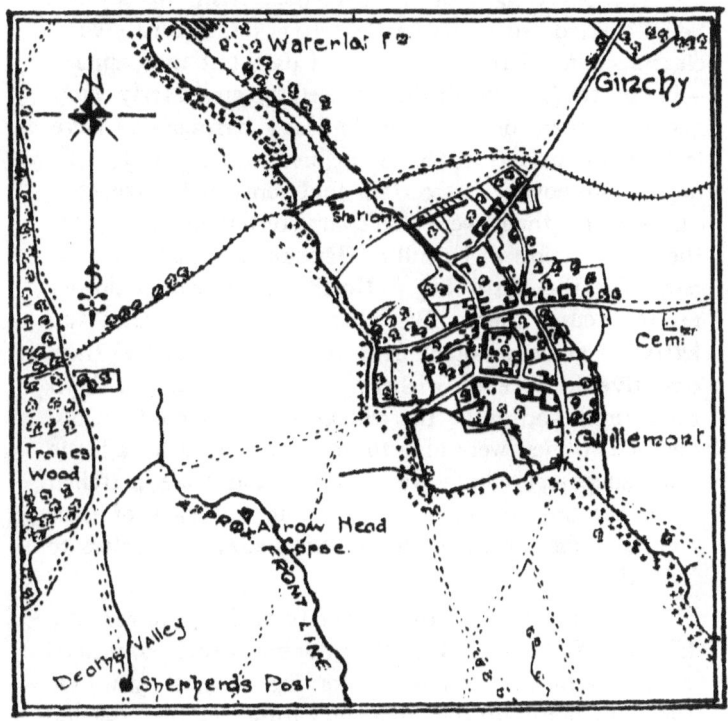

telephone communication with Brigade Headquarters. The right company had also established touch with the French according to programme. The position, therefore, on the afternoon of the 8th was: the right had succeeded and consolidated; the left had succeeded to some extent, but was cut off; the centre had failed to get forward.

The brave fight of the Liverpool Irish will always be associated with this battle. It is difficult to give a clear account of their actions that day, but they appear —in the thick cloud of dust caused by an easterly wind and the smoke of the enemy's heavy barrage—to have lost direction and to have inclined too much to the north. Moreover, it is certain that some of the trenches captured by them were not completely mopped up, for they were found to be full of Germans by the two companies of the 1/4th Loyal North Lancs. who followed up to occupy them. But there is no doubt that the battalion made a gallant fight and actually reached their objective in face of withering machine gun fire from their right and from the village of Guillemont. Only one or two men were able to make their way back; the remaining survivors were captured and were marched next day up the slope to Ginchy in full view of their comrades on the other side of the valley—powerless to help them.

In the evening of the same day orders were received from the XIII. Corps that the attack was to be continued at 4-20 a.m. the following morning—August 9th. On the right the objective was the capture of the trenches in front of those taken during the day; the objective on the left was the village of Guillemont. The Order of Battle was as follows :—The 165th Infantry Brigade on the right had the 1/7th King's Liverpools with one company of the 1/6th Liverpools in the front line; the remaining three companies of the 1/6th Liverpools in support, and the 1/9th Liverpools in reserve. The 166th

Infantry Brigade on the left had in the front line the Liverpool Scottish and the 1/5th Loyal North Lancs.; in support the 1/5th South Lancs., and in reserve the 1/5th King's Own Royal Lancasters.

For this attack there was no preliminary bombardment, but at 4-20 a.m. the barrage opened. In the centre the Liverpool Scottish moved off, following close under the barrage, and got within a few yards of the enemy trenches, to find that the wire had not been successfully cut. In spite of most gallant attempts to cut their way through, the obstacle proved impenetrable and the Officer Commanding, after leading his men a second time to the attack—in which he himself was wounded—finding it impossible to make headway, ordered a return to the original line. On the left the 1/5th Loyal North Lancs., owing to the lateness of the hour at which orders were received; to the narrowness and crowded condition of the trenches, due to reliefs; and to the heavy casualties to officers, were unable to get into position until after 5 a.m. In spite of this, and in spite of the fact that the artillery barrage had lifted at 4-23 a.m. as arranged, they made a most gallant assault. They were, however, unable to reach the German trenches, and were compelled to fall back to their starting point. Similar causes and similar difficulties hindered the success of the 165th Brigade on the right. The attack was gallantly pressed, but it failed, and the days following were spent in improving the trenches and consolidating the ground won.

On the 12th August, the French attacked the Angle Wood—Maltzhorn Ravine, and the 165th Infantry Brigade was ordered to co-operate by advancing their line on the right and by clearing the enemy out of Cochrane

Alley. Two companies of the 1/9th Liverpools made the attack, with the remaining companies in support and the 1/5th Liverpools in local reserve. The two leading companies attacked in two waves over about 400 yards of open ground, and when close to their objective were met by the enemy in the open, and fierce hand-to-hand fighting took place. But the 1/9th Liverpools, driving the enemy before them, captured their objective and proceeded to consolidate. Meantime the bombers had successfully cleared Cochrane Alley and had formed a new block in front of the previous one. Unfortunately for our success, however, the French failed to capture the Ravine, with the result that the 1/9th Liverpools were outflanked and badly enfiladed from the right. They held on doggedly, but, as their position became obviously untenable, they were withdrawn.

The following telegram was received next day from the Earl of Cavan, Commanding XIV. Corps :—

"The Corps Commander wishes you to express to the companies engaged last night his admiration, and that of the French who saw them, for the gallant and strenuous fight they put up.

"Had the Ravine been captured by the French there is no doubt our objective could have been realised. "13th August, 1916."

The Division, with the exception of the Artillery, was relieved on the night of the 14th/15th of August and moved back, to rest and re-fit, West of Abbeville. Casualties during the heavy fighting in which it had been engaged, were severe, but the bravery and courage of the troops in the attack were magnificent, and the Lancashire characteristic, dogged determination, was never better shown. Any ground gained was seldom lost. During this period from July 30th to August 16th our line was advanced 500 yards on the right and 300 yards on the left. 13,000 yards of new trenches were dug by the Division during this time and over 3,000 yards were deepened and improved.

On the night of the 4th/5th September the Division came back into the line, and the 165th and 166th Infantry Brigades with two companies of the 1/4th South Lancs. (Pioneers) and the 1/1st (now 419th) Field Company, R.E., relieved Brigades of the 24th Division from a point mid-way between High Wood and Delville Wood, across the Longueval-Flers road, round the front of Delville Wood to Ale Alley, East of Delville Wood. On the 7th September the 164th Infantry Brigade, with a Company of the 1/4th South Lancs. and the 2/2nd (now 422nd) Field Company, R.E., relieved a Brigade of the 7th Division in the line from Ale Alley to Ginchy Avenue, south-east of Delville Wood.

The situation here was a peculiar one. The enemy was still holding on with determination to about 20 yards of the north-east corner of Delville Wood, and Ginchy was still in his hands, having been re-captured from the 7th Division a week after its capture by them. To the south and south-east a line running to the north of Guillemont was held by the 16th and 36th Divisions.

THE BATTLE OF SEPTEMBER 9TH, 1916.

Orders were received from the XV. Corps that the attack would be renewed at 4-45 in the afternoon of the 9th September. The 16th Division of the XIV. Corps were to attack on the right of the Division and capture Ginchy, and the 1st Division of the III. Corps were to

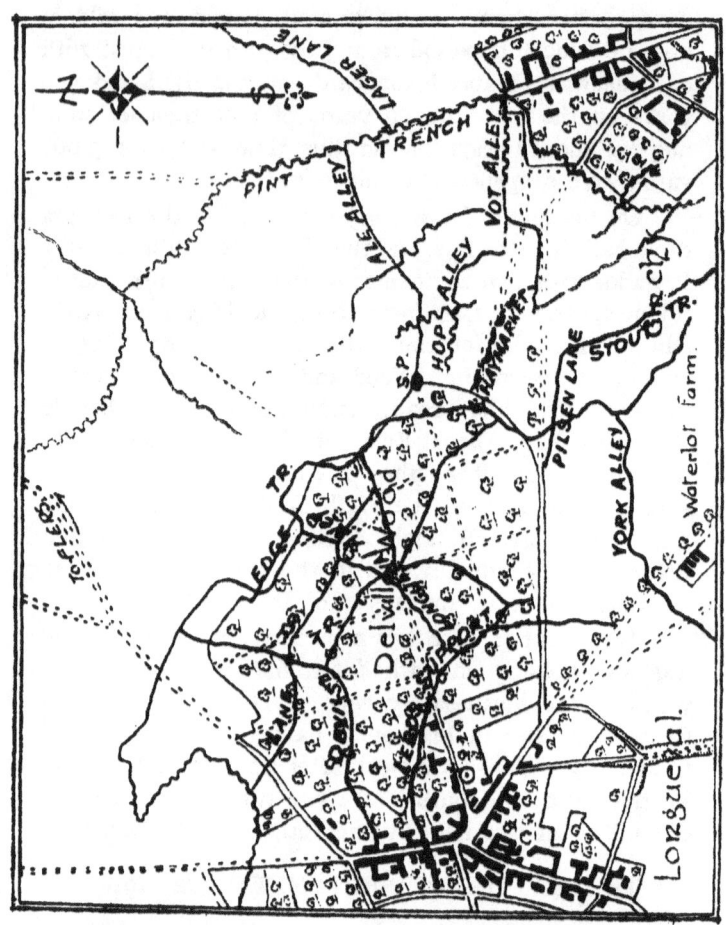

attack on the left. From 7 a.m. on the morning of the 9th the Heavy and Field Artillery commenced a deliberate bombardment and continued it until zero hour, when the Field Artillery put down a creeping barrage, behind which the Infantry were to advance. The enemy replied to this bombardment by shelling heavily our support trenches, and by gas shell on the batteries.

The task of the 164th Infantry Brigade was first to take a line of trenches running roughly from the outskirts of Ginchy to the east corner of Delville Wood, and, secondly, to capture Hop Alley and Ale Alley—which ran at right angles to our front line—as far as the junction of Ale Alley with Pint Trench, and then at right angles south along Pint Trench to Lager Lane. The 166th Infantry Brigade was to co-operate with the 164th Infantry Brigade by making a bombing attack on Ale Alley from the north-east corner of Delville Wood. The 165th Infantry Brigade had a separate task, which must be described later.

At the appointed hour two companies of the 1/4th Loyal North Lancs. left their trenches and, following close behind the barrage, attacked Hop Alley. They were followed immediately by the 2/5th Lancashire Fusiliers, who attacked Ale Alley and Pint Trench and attempted to consolidate them and to construct a strong point at the junction of the two trenches. Meanwhile a battalion of the 166th Infantry Brigade made a bombing attack on Ale Alley from the north, according to programme.

It soon became apparent, however, that the general attack was not going to succeed. Hop Alley, the first place to be taken, proved to be very much stronger than had been anticipated, and was held by a large garrison with many machine guns. Moreover, an unknown disguised trench—afterwards named Haymarket—deceived the leading wave as to its objective and caused some moments of disastrous delay. At one time it was reported that the 1/4th Loyal North Lancs. had captured Hop Alley, but, if the report was true, they must have been unable to hold it, and, in spite of most determined efforts, were compelled to occupy shell holes in front, after losing heavily in Officers and men. The Lancashire Fusiliers fared no better, for they were compelled to return to Pilsen Lane after having approached to within 20 yards of Hop Alley, their casualties having been very severe.

Further north, however, the 165th Infantry Brigade had been successful. They were co-operating with the 2nd Battalion King's Royal Rifles in an attack upon Wood Lane, the sunken road running between Longueval and High Wood. The 1/5th Liverpools, with one company of the 1/6th Liverpools in support, carried out this operation by means of a bombing attack up the trench, and in 15 minutes they had reached their objective and were consolidating and constructing strong points. They were also in touch with the 1st Division on their left.

Two days later, another attack upon Hop Alley and Ale Alley was made by the 1/4th King's Own Royal Lancasters of 164th Infantry Brigade. The attack was in the nature of a surprise and took place without artillery preparation. It failed, however, as the previous attack had failed. Machine gun and rifle fire from Hop Alley and also from Lager Lane, inflicted such casualties as to make progress impossible.

On the nights of the 10th and 12th of September the Division was relieved by the New Zealand Division on the left and on the right by the 41st Division, and withdrew to the Ribemont area. It was, however, destined to have but a short rest, and on the night of the 17th September it relieved the 41st Division in front of Flers, having the 21st Division on the right and the New Zealand Division on the left. The 165th Infantry Brigade took over the front with the 166th Brigade in support in the western edge of Flers village, and the 164th Brigade in reserve in Savoy and Carlton Trenches.

THE BATTLE OF SEPTEMBER 25TH, 1916.

The Division was to take part in the general attack along the whole front of the Fourth Army arranged to take place at 12-35 p.m. on the 25th September. The objective allotted to it was the Gird Trench and the Gird Support, north-west of Gueudecourt, from the point at which they were cut by the road running from the Pilgrim's Way to the west end of Gueudecourt, to their junction with the Gueudecourt—Factory Corner Road.

The attack was to be made in two stages: the first objective was the Factory Corner Road, from the corner to the point where it met Gird Trench and Gird Support. Gird Trench and Gird Support were also to be taken as far as the right Divisional boundary. Touch was to be obtained with the New Zealand Division at Factory Corner. The second objective was the remaining portion of the Factory Corner Road as far as the cross road at the north-west edge of Gueudecourt, where touch was to be obtained with the 21st Division. The 165th Infantry Brigade was ordered to carry out the attack, and it detailed the 1/7th Liverpools on the right, the 1/6th Liverpools in the centre, and the 1/9th Liverpools on the left. These battalions were to assault; the 1/5th Liverpools formed the reserve.

At 12-35 p.m. the first wave of the infantry left the trenches and advanced to the assault, closely following the creeping barrage. On this occasion the infantry kept closer to the barrage than ever before, preferring to suffer some casualties from possible short shells from their own gunners, rather than to run the risk of allowing the barrage to get away from them and of being compelled to face the enemy's uninterrupted machine gun and rifle fire, as had on more than one occasion happened previously. The result was eminently successful. Thanks to the excellence of the barrage and to the splendid dash of the infantry in keeping up to it, the enemy was unable to bring his machine guns into action in time, and the whole of the first objective was captured with few casualties. Quickly the work of consolidation and reorganisation was carried on, while the barrage remained stationary in front. When presently the barrage once more moved forward the 1/7th and part of the 1/6th Liverpools advanced closely behind it, and the second objective was taken.

For some time, however, the situation was critical. Touch could not be obtained with the 21st Division on the right, and it was not known if Gueudecourt had been taken. Moreover, touch had not yet been obtained with the New Zealand Division on the left, but it was known that they were holding Factory Corner, and touch was eventually obtained with them at 8-30 that evening.

At 6-30 p.m. it was known that the 21st Division had not succeeded in their attempt to capture Gueudecourt. This meant that our right flank was dangerously exposed, and the 1/7th Liverpools at once began to construct strong points on this flank. When darkness came both they and the 1/6th Liverpools were reinforced—each by a company of the 1/5th Liverpools—and by daybreak the position was secure.

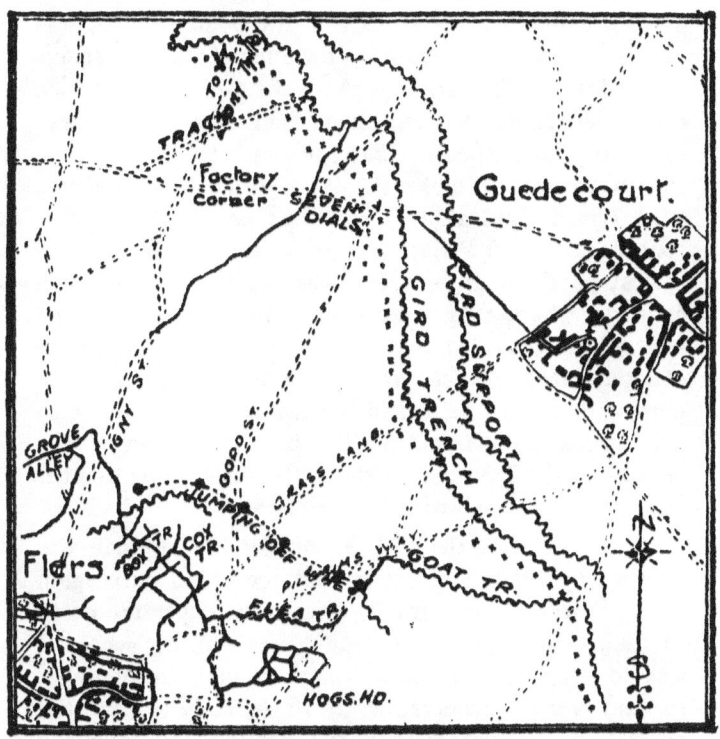

SCALE 1/20.0.00

On the 27th September the Division was ordered to exploit the success thus gained by capturing—in conjunction with the New Zealand Division—the Gird Trench and Gird Support north of Factory Corner as far as the point where these trenches cut the Factory Corner—Ligny—Tilloy Road. The task was allotted to the 164th Infantry Brigade, which ordered the 1/8th Liverpools (Irish) to capture the objective. For seven hours previous to the attack a heavy bombardment was carried out, and at 2-20 p.m. the Field Artillery barrage came down. The Irish showed the same dash which the other Liverpool battalions had shown two days previously, and when the barrage was lifted at 2-23 p.m. they were close up under it. At 2-30 they had captured Gird Trench, and at 3-15 they had captured and were consolidating Gird Support, with the enemy in full retreat on the Ligny—Tilloy Road and across the open country, where they were caught by our barrage and suffered heavily. At 3-50 p.m. the enemy attempted to counter-attack, but he was caught in our barrage once more and suffered further heavy casualties without being able to reach the trenches the Irish were holding. The attacks of the Division on the 25th and 27th September were thus crowned with signal success.

On the night of the 28th September the Division was relieved by the 41st Division and proceeded once again to the Buire—Ribemont area prior to its departure north to take over a portion of the Ypres Salient, where it was to remain for so many months, and, incidentally, to add very considerably to its already substantial reputation. Before leaving the Somme the following message was received —:

"55th Division,

"As the Division is now leaving the Fourth Army I desire to express to all ranks my gratitude for the good work that has been done, and my congratulations on the results achieved.

"The hard fighting in which it took part about Guillemont and Delville Wood during August and September was a severe strain on all ranks, and the progress made in these areas reflects great credit on all concerned. When put into the line for the third time to carry out the attack near Gueudecourt on September 25th, the Division exhibited a spirit of gallantry and endurance which was wholly admirable and which resulted in the capture of all the objectives allotted.

"The co-operation and support of the Divisional Artillery was all that could be desired.

"I regret that the Division is leaving the Fourth Army, and trust that on some future occasion I may have the good fortune to find it again under my command.

"H. RAWLINSON,
General,
Commanding Fourth Army.
Headquarters, Fourth Army,
4th October, 1916."

CHAPTER III.

YPRES, JULY 31ST AND SEPTEMBER 20TH.

The Division was now transferred to the Second Army (Sir Herbert Plumer) and relieved the 29th Division in the Ypres Salient in October, 1916. Except for two periods of rest—in January, and after the battle of July 31st—it remained in the Salient until the end of September, 1917. The portion of the line taken over by the Division ran from Wieltje to the south of Railway Wood. During the first few months the sector was what might be called a " quiet " sector. Both the enemy and ourselves were tired after the strenuous work of the Somme and required, and obtained, rest. Then, the Division being thoroughly rested and re-equipped, things commenced to wake up and a certain liveliness began. This liveliness continued with ever growing intensity until the end of July, when the long-expected offensive was launched. During the period from October to July 31st the Division had, naturally, become thoroughly acquainted with the section of the enemy line in front of it, and so well had it acquitted itself in the continuous raids and harassments, so completely had it gained the measure of its task, and the confidence of the supreme command, that it was chosen to carry out the assault on its own front—an honour which it both appreciated and entirely vindicated.

To give even a brief account of the constant raids and minor operations undertaken by the Division during the ten months of its occupation of the salient prior to the battle of the 31st July, would take more space than can be afforded. It may be mentioned, however, that while the Division as a unit was not actively engaged in the June operation which resulted in the capture, by the Second Army, of the Messines Ridge, the Divisional Artillery co-operated in the attack and was subsequently complimented by the Army Commander upon its efficient work.

THE BATTLE OF JULY 31ST, 1917.

The objective of what was called the Third Battle of Ypres was the capture of the enemy's Gheluvelt—Langemarck system. It was also hoped to obtain a footing upon the Gravenstafel spur, but this was not to be pushed, and was contingent upon circumstances. It was, in fact, not intended to attack any position in which strong resistance was offered by the enemy other than the Gheluvelt—Langemarck line.

The attack was to be made by the Fifth Army—to which the Division had been transferred—in conjunction with the Second Army and the First French Army. The XIX. Corps was to attack with the 15th Division on the right and the 55th Division on the left. The 16th and 36th Divisions were in reserve. The XVIII. Corps was to attack on the left of the 55th Division.

The 55th Division was to attack with the 165th Infantry Brigade on the right, the 166th Infantry Brigade on the left, and the 164th Infantry Brigade in reserve. All units were to be in their zero positions by 2 a.m. on zero day. The attack was to be made in three stages:—

1st Objective.—At zero (3-50 a.m.) the leading two battalions each of the 165th and 166th Infantry Brigades were to advance and to capture the enemy's front line system of trenches up to and including the *Blue Line*. (See Map).

2nd Objective.—At zero, plus 1 hour 15 minutes, the remaining two battalions, each of 165th and 166th Infantry Brigades, were to capture and consolidate the enemy's second line system (Stutzpunkt Line) up to and including the *Black Line*.

At zero, plus 3 hours 33 minutes, the 166th Infantry Brigade was to advance its left to capture Canvas and Capitol Trenches up to Border House, if these had not already been captured. This advance was to be made in conjunction with a corresponding advance by the 39th Division to a line running approximately parallel to the Steenbeke and 300 yards east of it.

3rd Objective.—At zero, plus 6 hours 20 minutes, the 164th Infantry Brigade was to pass through the 165th and 166th Infantry Brigades on the Black Line and proceed to capture the enemy's third line system (Gheluvelt-Langemarck Line) up to the *Green Line*.

The preliminary move forward of units took place on July 29th and the night 29th/30th, and the following night saw the closing up of units into their battle positions. Thanks to an almost entire absence of hostile shelling, the concentration forward was completed without incident.

The weather during the whole of June and during the greater part of July had been ideal weather for campaigning purposes. Unfortunately, on Sunday, July 29th, a particularly heavy thunderstorm filled up the shell holes and turned roads and tracks into a morass. The succeeding days were dull and hazy, making the completion of the artillery preparation peculiarly difficult.

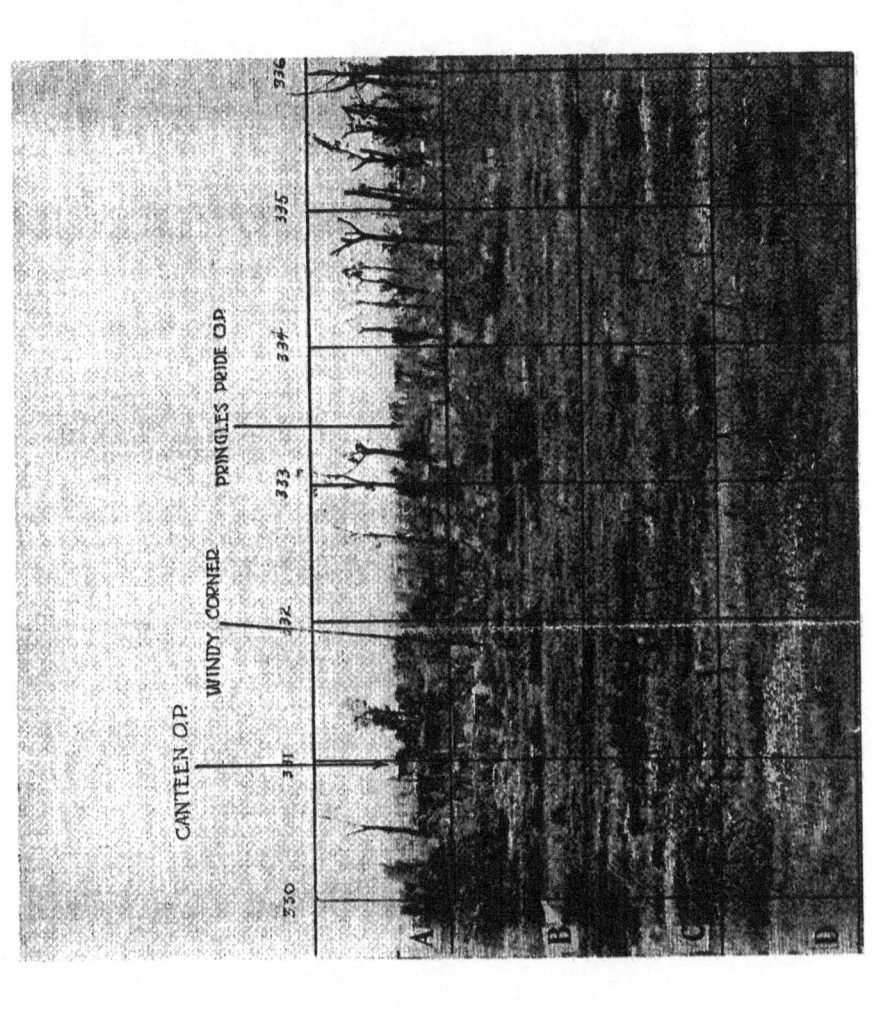

Photograph showing the objectives to be captured by the Division on July 31st, 1917. All these objectives were taken.
(Hill 37 lies behind and to the left of Iberian).

and typical Flanders weather conditions prevailed on the morning of the 31st—the moment chosen for the attack. Low lying clouds which made ærial observation and co-operation as difficult as could be imagined ; a dampness of atmosphere, threatening rain at any moment ; a half sodden ground, greasy and depressing ; such was the luck of the weather at 3-50 a.m. on the 31st of July, 1917, when the artillery barrage opened. Not since the war began had so intense a barrage been put down, and of its wonderful effectiveness all ranks in the line bore eloquent testimony.

Immediately the barrage opened the leading waves left their trenches for the assault. The morning was particularly dark and the men experienced some difficulty in keeping their proper direction. Advancing close behind the barrage the 1/5th and 1/6th King's Liverpools captured the enemy front system up to the Blue Line without special incident. The enemy's machine guns were found to be very active from Plum Farm—a point well beyond the Blue Line and through which our defensive barrage ran. In spite of the fact that our barrage was on the Farm, it was at once attacked and captured with the three machine guns which it contained. (The capture of this strong point before the advance from the Blue Line considerably assisted the advance of the 1/7th and 1/9th Liverpools to the Black Line). The two leading battalions of the 166th Infantry Brigade—the 1/5th Royal Lancs. and the 1/5th North Lancs. met with equal success, and the 1/5th Royal Lancs. were reported to be digging in on the Blue Line at 4-45 a.m., and prisoners were already coming in.

At 5-5 a.m., as arranged, the remaining battalions of the 165th and 166th Brigades—the 1/7th and 1/9th

King's Liverpools, and the 1/10th Liverpool Scottish and 1/5th South Lancs.—advanced to the capture of the Black Line. This was not effected, however, without serious opposition. Heavy machine gun fire from Square Farm, in the 15th Divisional area, considerably delayed the 1/7th Liverpools, and the Farm had eventually to be captured by them. The garrison of 130 men surrendered and threw down their arms. They afterwards ran off to the right with their hands up and were all taken prisoners by the 46th Infantry Brigade.

Meanwhile the 1/9th Liverpools on the left had been held up by heavy fire from Bank Farm. This, however, with the assistance of a Tank, was captured, and the advance to the objective continued. But the Liverpool Scottish and the 1/5th South Lancs. were experiencing severe opposition from Capricorn Trench, Pond Farm, and Spree Farm, and the 1/5th North Lancs. were despatched to their support. The attack was pressed home, and by 7 a.m. Capricorn was in complete possession of the Scottish who were in touch with the 1/5th South Lancs. on the right. The enemy, however, was heavily disputing our advance from every available position in and beyond the Black Line, and very severe fighting took place before the objective on this part of the front was eventually reached. At 9 a.m. touch was gained with 165th Infantry Brigade, and the whole of the Black Line was believed to be occupied and in our possession.

This, however, proved to be a mistake. Spree Farm was still in the hands of the enemy and was not finally cleared until the arrival of troops of the 164th Infantry Brigade. Pond Farm, too, was causing considerable trouble, and the work of consolidation, and the construc-

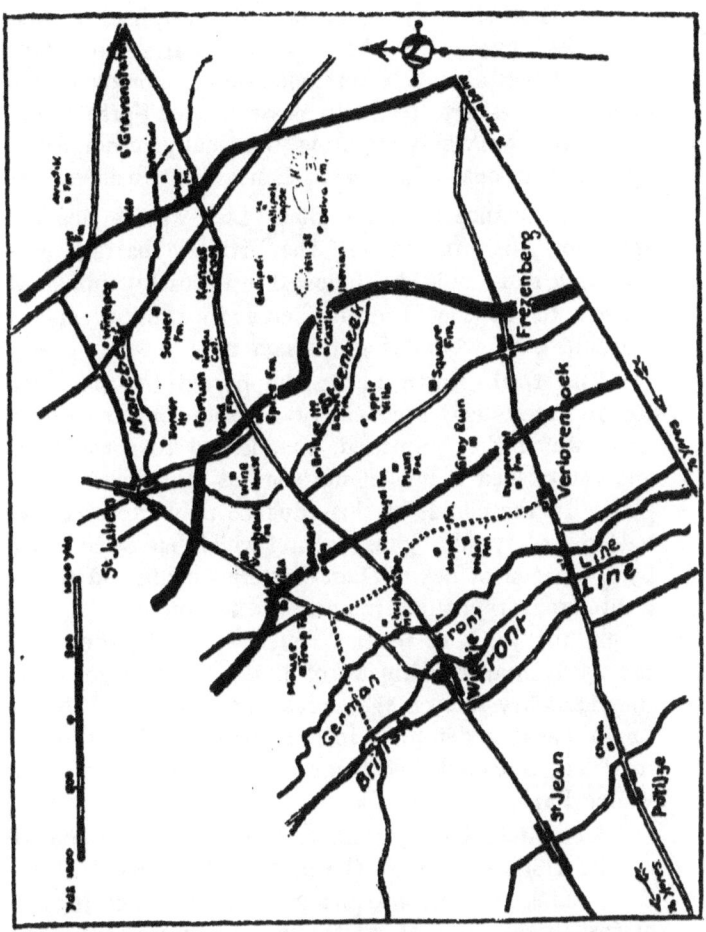

tion of supporting points, though carried on vigorously, was fiercely disputed.

At 10-10 a.m., as ordered, the 164th Infantry Brigade advanced to the capture of the final objective—the Green

Line. On their way up they had sustained serious casualties, principally from Square Farm—to which reference has already been made—and, moreover, had found it necessary to obtain possession of Spree Farm, which, after very sharp fighting, was finally accomplished by two platoons of the 2/5th Lancashire Fusiliers.

The advance from the Black Line was carried out according to programme. The artillery barrage was excellent and could be followed up closely, though it proved to be insufficiently dense to prevent enemy machine guns from firing through it.

The 1/4th North Lancs., supported by the 1/4th Royal Lancasters, successfully advanced to the Green Line, which they captured, commenced to consolidate, and established a line of outposts as laid down in the plan. In the course of this advance they captured five batteries of 77 m.m. guns, each of which had to be taken by a platoon attack. These batteries continued to fire until the last possible moment—when our troops were within 100 yards of them. Touch was established with the 45th Infantry Brigade of the 15th Division about the Boundary line on the Green line. The 1/4th North Lancs. were not definitely in touch with the battalion on their left, but could see them on the high ground about Wurst Farm and Aviatik.

Meantime, the 2/5th Lancashire Fusiliers, supported by the 1/8th Liverpools (Irish) had also arrived at the Green Line, but, in consequence of the fierce fighting and of casualties sustained on the way up, were very weak in numbers. Wurst Farm was reached and an Officer patrolled as far as Aviatik. On the left of our men the 1/6th Cheshires had reached the Green Line, but owing, it is understood, to the fact that the battalion on their left had been unable to advance, the position about Wurst Farm and north-west of it was subjected to heavy fire from the left flank and left rear, and the line was compelled to fall back by Winnipeg. Later it was learnt that the 118th Infantry Brigade, on our left, had been forced back to the line Border House—thence north-west along the line of the Steenbeke. Arrangements were made by the 2/5th Lancashire Fusiliers and the 1/8th Liverpools to bend back the line from the position occupied to Border House, and the two battalions on the right were immediately notified in order that they might adjust their line so as to conform with this movement.

Whilst these dispositions were being made, and a party of reinforcements had been collected and sent up to strengthen the wired line of gun positions to the south-west of Schuler Farm, a heavy counter-attack developed, supported by an intense artillery barrage and machine gun fire. This attack was directed from the right and the left simultaneously, and several battalions were used by the enemy. The principal artillery fire on the right came from the direction of Zonnebeke, and was in enfilade. This counter-attack made a further withdrawal necessary, and after magnificent rearguard fighting which caused the heaviest losses to the enemy, the 164th Infantry Brigade fell back to the Black Line. Here during the night the Brigade, which had suffered heavily, was relieved by the 165th and 166th Infantry Brigades, and withdrew to the old British front line.

Shortly after eight o'clock in the evening the rain, which had been threatening all day, came down steady and remorseless, and continued with varying intensity for weeks. The weather conditions, indeed, could not have been worse and the elements seemed to be throwing in all their weight on the side of the enemy. Shell holes became feet deep in water; mud changed from dough to slime; everything was discouraging, disappointing and depressing enough to break the spirit of any but the British soldier. Surely never in history did men fight under more appalling conditions.

The Division had received orders that the Black Line was to be held at all costs and that all ground now held was to be consolidated in preparation for a renewal of the attack. The night of the 31st July and the day following were spent in this work. Frequently the enemy showed signs of launching counter-attacks, but these were effectively dispersed by artillery and machine gun fire. At 7-15 on the morning of August 1st a message was received from the 165th Infantry Brigade stating that the situation was now satisfactory and that the Black Line was strongly established. A very heavy counter-attack upon our positions at Pommern Redoubt at 1-40 p.m. on the 2nd August was splendidly repulsed, with very heavy losses to the enemy, after which the Division was relieved by the 36th Division, and proceeded to the Recques area, near St. Omer, for rest and training. The relief was completed at 4 a.m. on August 4th, with the exception of the Artillery and the Pioneers, who remained in the line for a further period.

The Division had fought well, as it was presently to learn from the higher authorities. All objectives had been taken and the subsequent withdrawal from the Green Line to the Black Line was forced upon it by circumstances for which it was not responsible. Very heavy losses were inflicted on the enemy, some 30 Officers and 600 other ranks had been taken prisoners, and many guns, trench mortars and machine guns were captured. The severity of the fighting is evidenced by our losses. The casualties from noon July 30th to noon August 4th were 168 Officers and 3,384 other ranks. But the Division had found itself.

On August 7th the moves of the Division into the Recques area were completed. Reinforcements began to arrive and intensive training was commenced and continued. On August 19th Field Marshal Sir Douglas Haig visited the Division. The period from August 7th to September 12th, when the Division returned to the line, was taken full advantage of. Athletic sports, a football tournament, cross country run, and a very successful Divisional Horse Show, provided variety and recreation during the training, and it was a Division thoroughly refreshed, rested, re-equipped, and in splendid spirits, which moved forward to the old area on the 12th September. During the period of its absence from the line two attempts by other Divisions had been made to advance from the Black Line, but each attempt had failed. Except for slight progress made in certain places, the portion of the line taken over by the Division on September 15th was identical to that held when it was relieved six weeks before. And it was now asked to capture the same objective—or practically the same—as that which it had captured originally on July 31st.

Extracts from the Operation Order issued at 11 a.m. on September 18th are of interest:—

"The Second and Fifth Armies are to resume the offensive on Z day, the date of which will be notified later.

"The attack of the V. Corps will be carried out by the 9th Division on the right and the 55th Division on the left.

"The 38th Division (XVIII. Corps) will be on the left of the 55th Division.

"It is the intention to capture and secure the final objective (Green Line), and to this end the whole strength of the Division will be devoted.

"The capture and retention of Hill 37 is of special importance."

There is no doubt that the Division was thoroughly " on its mettle "—to use an old north country expression —and was determined that Hill 37 and Schuler Farm should be permanently inscribed on its Battle Honours.

On the night of September 19th/20th all units closed up into their final assembly positions for the attack, and to the chargin of everbody rain once again immediately began to fall. It was exasperating, to say the least. The 164th and 165th Infantry Brigades closed up to an area east of the Stutzpunkt Line, with the leading waves aligned on a line of posts in shell holes which were already in our hands. To each of these Brigades was attached a battalion of the 166th Infantry Brigade, and these battalions—the 1/5th Loyal North Lancs. and the 1/5th Royal Lancasters—were assembled in the old German front line system. In rear of these again were the remaining two battalions of the 166th Infantry Brigade— 1/5th South Lancs. and Liverpool Scottish—assembled as Divisional Reserve under the Brigadier-General Commanding the 166th Infantry Brigade. The Field Companies R.E. and Pioneers were assembled in Ypres and on the Canal Bank north of it.

The move up of the leading battalions to the position of deployment was well carried out, in spite of great difficulties. The night was very dark and wet, and the front of the deployment was an ill-defined line of shell hole posts. The success of the deployment was due to the very careful reconnaissance beforehand, and to the careful way in which flanks of platoons were marked by notice boards and tape. Units also had been extensively practised in night deployment during the training period.

THE BATTLE OF SEPTEMBER 20TH, 1917.

Zero was fixed at 5-40 a.m. on September 20th, and at that hour punctually the barrage opened on the enemy's front line. This barrage was the conclusion of an intense bombardment by all calibres, which had commenced at 3 a.m. on the previous day. The leading waves moved forward to the assault and formed up close under the barrage, which made its first lift at 5-45 a.m. and moved 50 yards at a time. The enemy's artillery retaliated with 4.2s. and 5.9s. at Zero or soon after, his fire falling on our front line of assembly and also on waves formed up in rear. The fire was effective until the rear waves had advanced and had closed up to those in front. (A prisoner stated subsequently that the tapes marking our assembly positions had been seen, and the attack expected.) Although the advance was carried out by the 164th and 165th Infantry Brigades in line with each other, the action of these two Brigades, and of the battalions attached to them from the 166th Infantry Brigade, is best described separately. The progress of the 165th Infantry Brigade on the right sector will, therefore, first be dealt with.

On going forward to the attack the two leading battalions were almost immediately met with heavy rifle and machine gun fire from Kaynorth, Iberian, Lens, and Gallipoli. Very severe fighting ensued, in which the whole of the two leading battalions became involved, and also some troops of the supporting battalions. Iberian and Kaynorth were, however, successfully captured at 6-45 a.m., Lens at 7-40 a.m. and Gallipoli soon after 8 a.m. Several smaller strong points in the neighbourhood of Hill 35, however, were still holding out and were inflicting severe casualties upon the attacking troops. Both the support battalions were drawn into the fighting before the Yellow Line was reached. At 9-45 a.m. two companies of the 1/5th North Lancs. Regiment were ordered to reinforce the 1/6th King's Liverpools and to attack Hill 37. About 11 a.m. two companies succeeded in capturing the Hill, but at 11-20 were counter-attacked and driven back. At 11-45 a.m. the 1/5th King's Liverpools reported that they were holding Ditch Trench but that no one was on their left, and the Germans appeared now to be holding Hill 37 in great strength.

Meanwhile, reports were received that small German posts were still holding out east of Hill 35 and were making all movement very difficult. The O.C. 1/9th King's Liverpools was, therefore, ordered to collect all available men and to form two mopping-up waves and thoroughly clear all this area so as to clear the way for an organised attack on Hill 37, which was to be undertaken as soon as the necessary reinforcements arrived. It was not until 2 p.m. that all the eastern side of Hill 35—including Suvla—was reported to be quite clear of the enemy. A counter-attack upon our front between 2 p.m. and 2-30 p.m. was frustrated by our artillery.

The two companies of the 1/5th South Lancs. Regt., which had been sent up to reinforce the Brigade, arrived about 2-30 p.m. They were ordered to attack Hill 37 from Hill 35, and all available men from the 1/6th and 1/9th King's Liverpools were ordered to co-operate in the attack. The 1/5th King's Liverpools were ordered to assault the Hill from the south as soon as the South Lancs. and 1/6th and 1/9th King's were seen to assault from the west. At 3-35 p.m. these troops were observed to be advancing on Hill 37 as ordered. No definite reports came back from the Hill until 5-10 p.m., when a message was received stating that Hill 37 had been captured and the position was being consolidated.

Meanwhile, a report had been received from the 164th Infantry Brigade on the left, stating that they had been driven back to the Red Dotted Line. At that time the 165th Infantry Brigade held Gallipoli, Keir Farm Dug-outs, and the Capitol. There was, however, a gap between Hill 37 and the Capitol. Two more companies of the 1/5th South Lancs. which had been sent up to reinforce, were, therefore, ordered to capture and hold Gallipoli Copse, and afterwards get in touch with Hill 37 on their right and the Capitol on their left. At 6-20 p.m. Gallipoli Copse was captured and the line linked up. The line then ran from Waterend House—where it joined up with the 9th Division—thence to Hill 37, Gallipoli Copse, Capitol, Keir Farm Dug-outs and Gallipoli, just north of which it joined up with the 164th Infantry Brigade.

Shortly after 5 p.m. another counter-attack on Hill 37, accompanied by a very heavy barrage, was delivered by the enemy in several waves from the Gravenstafel Ridge about Boetleer. This was beaten back with very severe loss to the enemy by our artillery, and by the fire of the machine guns in position near Keir Farm, which took it in enfilade. At 7-30 p.m. two companies of the Liverpool Scottish were sent up as reinforcements. They were ordered to move up to a position just west of Hill 37, and to hold themselves in readiness to make immediate counter-attack on the Hill, should the enemy by any chance succeed in re-capturing it.

The position gained was consolidated in depth ; every German strong point and concrete dug-out garrisoned ; a continuous trench was dug all along the front with strong points pushed out ; numerous supporting points were made behind, and troops posted at various points ready to counter-attack immediately. Machine guns were posted so as to afford mutual support to each other, and to bring a heavy concentration of fire in front of Hill 37; and all uninjured machine guns captured from the enemy were got into action by men of our Infantry, who had been specially trained to their use. Such is the account of the day's work of the Brigade on the right sector. It is now time to record what happened on the left.

As in the case of the right Brigade, the assaulting battalions of the 164th Infantry Brigade, immediately upon advancing, came under very severe rifle and machine gun fire from the front and from both flanks. On the right the hostile barrage caused the 1/4th Loyal North Lancs. to close up with the 1/4th Royal Lancasters, who were in front of them, and they became involved in the fighting earlier than had been anticipated. In fact, they became engaged—and suffered considerable losses—in the neighbourhood of Aisne Farm, which the 1/4th Royal Lancasters had swept past in the assault but had inadequately mopped up. From this stage onwards the two right battalions became more or less intermingled, and the heavy machine gun fire to which they were subjected from the right rendered re-organisation difficult.

The 2/5th Lancashire Fusiliers, advancing in the centre, came under very heavy fire both from the front and from the left flank, this latter coming from an enemy post north of Hanebeek. So heavy was this fire that before this battalion had reached Schuler galleries, its first objective, something like 50 per cent. of its strength had become casualties. The experience of the left battalion—the 1/8th Liverpools (Irish)—was very similar to that of the Fusiliers, and their advance was even more disorganised in consequence. Both the reserve companies of this battalion had been thrown into the fighting before the northern end of Schuler galleries— which was part of their first objective—had been gained. It is probable that the barrage had been lost before the Irish arrived at the northern end of Schuler galleries, and it was only after stiff fighting, and after the southern galleries had already been occupied by the 2/5th Lancs. Fusiliers, that these defences were finally reduced and occupied. The Fusiliers subsequently pushed on under the barrage, and elements of the battalion reached the Green Line, but not in sufficient force to hold it, and connection with these advanced elements could not be maintained. The 1/8th Liverpools (Irish) had failed in their original attacks on Schuler Farm owing to hostile fire from Cross Cotts, Kansas House area.

Shortly after 10 a.m. the enemy were observed to be massing for a counter-attack in the Nile–Fokker Farm area. The Artillery were informed, and the enemy, to the estimated number of 500, were cut to pieces by our barrage and machine gun fire. A second attempt a few hours later, made also by about 500 men, was similarly dealt with. The German casualties in each of these attempts were appalling.

On the right, the 1/4th Loyal North Lancs. had suffered heavily from machine gun fire from the right flank, and a portion of the battalion having become involved in the capture of Gallipoli, only small parties reached the leading lines of the 1/4th Royal Lancasters who were occupying the dotted Red Line. These parties were not sufficiently strong and could not continue the advance. Moreover, elements of the reserve battalion—the 1/5th King's Own Royal Lancasters—had become intermingled with other units, and although the Officer Commanding had been in touch with his assaulting battalions—the 1/4th North Lancs. and the 1/4th Royal Lancasters—the difficulty of keeping control over his unit in the unspeakably heavy ground, together with the heavy fire to which they were for the whole time subjected, had prevented his unit from being thrown in at the right moment to enable the attack to be continued. The 1/5th Royal Lancasters were, therefore, concentrated in the neighbourhood of Loos, to be in readiness for any hostile counter-attack.

Considerable obscurity reigned for some time as to the condition of affairs at Schuler Farm. At 11-10 a.m. a message from the 38th Division stated that they had a report that Schuler Farm had been taken. At 2-50 p.m. the 164th Infantry Brigade reported that this report was untrue—Schuler Farm was not taken. At 4-25 p.m. definite information was received that the Farm was still in the hands of the enemy, who were considerably harassing our troops by machine gun fire from the Farm. As a matter of fact Schuler Farm held out until 4-30 p.m. the following afternoon, when it was captured after stiff fighting by the 1/8th Liverpool Irish.

The situation at 8-15 p.m. on the 20th was as follows: The left Brigade—164th—held the Dotted Red Line in strength, with posts in shell holes and otherwise as far forward as the Green Line,—touch with which had, however, been temporarily lost. The Capitol was held and also Gallipoli Copse. Hill 37 was in our hands, together with the Snag east of it, and we joined up by a series of short trenches to Waterend House on the right of the Divisional front. The assault had been a success. Hill 37, which for so long had withstood all attempts to capture it, was ours, and was firmly held. The Green Line, too, for the most part, was ours, and the troublesome Schuler Farm was to fall to us the next day. At 11-45 p.m. a telegram was received from the Army Commander congratulating all ranks and all arms for their splendid efforts, and at midnight a telegram, couched in similar terms, from the Corps Commander, congratulated all ranks on the day's work.

Late in the afternoon of the next day, the 21st, a very heavy enemy barrage opened out all along the ridge from Hill 37 to Hill 35, and it was evident that a desperate attempt was to be made to re-capture the vantage ground gained by us the previous day. On Hill 37 a very heavy attack developed. The enemy advanced in dense waves, followed by small columns. All roads and approaches were heavily shelled by the enemy, and the attack was furiously pressed. But our men stood firm. In a few places the Germans gained a footing in our defences, but were vigorously driven back, and shortly after 8 p.m. the attack collapsed. Hill 37 was still ours, and remained ours.

A similar counter-attack north of Gallipoli at the Keir Farm dug-outs met with a temporary success, and here again the enemy broke through. He was, however, speedily ousted, and we regained, and retained, what we had so hardly won the day before. At 11-20 p.m. that night the General sent out a wire of congratulation to all ranks on defeating the enemy's counter-attacks. In addition to the ground gained, the Division captured two Officers and 245 other ranks, one field gun and 20 machine guns. Our casualties from noon on the 19th to noon on the 24th September, when the Division was relieved, amounted to 127 Officers and 2,603 other ranks. The casualties inflicted upon the enemy were very heavy indeed.

The relief of the Division by the 39th Division commenced on the night 22nd/23rd September, and was completed by 6 a.m. on the 24th. On the 25th September it proceeded south to join the Third Army, and relieved the 35th Division in the line south of Cambrai. The Command of the 35th Divisional front passed to the G.O.C. 55th Division at 10 a.m. on the 3rd of October.

AUCHEL, *April, 1918.*

Top row: Major R. P. Power, O.B.E., Capt. R. L. Dobell, Rev. J. O. Coop, D.S.O., Major Sir E. H. Preston, Bart., D.S.O., M.C., Major Hon. E. C. Lascelles, D.S.O., M.C.

Bottom row: Major M. H. Milner, D.S.O., M.V.O., Lt.-Col. S. H. Eden, C.M.G., D.S.O., Major-General Sir H. S. Jeudwine, K.C.B., Lt.-Col. T. R. C. Price, C.M.G., D.S.O., Capt. G. Surtees, M.C.

CHAPTER IV.

CAMBRAI. NOVEMBER 20TH AND 30TH, 1917.

The portion of the line taken over by the Division ran, roughly, from west of Honnecourt Wood, north-east of Epehy, to New Post, south-east of the villages Lempire—Ronssoy; a frontage of about 8,000 yards. The sector was as unlike the old Ypres sector as could well be imagined. Instead of a continuous trench system, strongly held and fiercely menaced, here was just a stretch of fortified posts with a connecting system. The Division held a front four times the length of that held at Ypres, and this frontage was soon to be even further extended.

The usual process of harassment commenced on the night of October 10th/11th, when a concentration shoot by the Heavy Artillery, Divisional Artillery, Trench Mortars, Stokes Mortars and Machine Guns was carried out upon selected objectives. These concentration shoots upon the enemy's defences and strong points were continued at frequent intervals throughout October and November, and caused much damage and disquiet to the enemy. On November 18th, at about 5-30 a.m., the enemy put down a severe Trench Mortar and Artillery barrage upon our front and, under cover of this barrage, entered our lines in three separate parties. A stubborn resistance was offered by our garrisons, and severe casualties were inflicted upon the enemy, whose forces were estimated to have exceeded 200. (This was subsequently confirmed by prisoners). A counter-attack was promptly organised by the support company in Ken Lane, which came into action over the open. As soon as the enemy observed this he retired with considerable precipitation, leaving four prisoners in our hands.

THE BATTLE OF NOVEMBER 20TH.

The operation undertaken by the Division on the 20th of November was undertaken in conjunction with, but entirely subsidiary to, the main attack in the North against the enemy's defences near Cambrai, known as the Hindenburg Line. The object of this operation on the part of the Division was to contain the enemy on our front, and to prevent him from moving troops northward. It may at once be stated that the object was attained.

The particular work entrusted to the Division was the attack, and, if possible, the retention of the important enemy defences of Gillemont Farm and the Knoll. It was not, however, intended to force the attack if the enemy offered serious resistance, nor was the retention of the two objectives at all costs contemplated. If necessary they were to be evacuated, the main object of containing the enemy having been attained. The extent of the front of attack from right to left was 2,500 yards, and it contained the two very strong positions above-mentioned. Only one Brigade was available to make the attack. The whole of the remainder of the Division was occupied in holding the very extended trench line. Consequently it was necessary to concentrate on the two main objectives, Gillemont Farm and the Knoll, and to trust to subsequent extension by bombing attacks to connect them up. The operation thus consisted of two simultaneous but almost independent attacks.

Zero hour was fixed for 6-20 a.m., and at that hour the Artillery barrage opened on the enemy's front line opposite Gillemont Farm, and 20 minutes later opened also upon the Knoll. The attack was carried out by the 164th Infantry Brigade; the 1/8th Liverpools (Irish) on the right, and the 2/5th Lancashire Fusiliers on the left, were to attack and capture the Knoll, and the 1/4th King's Own Royal Lancasters were to take Gillemont Farm. To these battalions the 1/5th Liverpools were attached as "Counter-attack Reserve," and were disposed as follows :—one company in Ken Lane–Sart Lane; one company in Doleful Post; one company in Fleeceall Post, and one company in Grafton Post.

At 6-22 a.m., as arranged, the Infantry for the attack on Gillemont Farm left their trenches and advanced to the assault; the two battalions attacking the Knoll were launched at 6-44 a.m., closing up to the creeping barrage. At 6-30 a.m. a dummy attack, with mechanical figures and a dummy Tank, was carried out from the Birdcage by the 1/9th Liverpool Regiment, and information subsequently received proved that these dummies providing, as was intended, excellent targets, attracted a very great deal of hostile fire and caused the enemy much useless wastage of ammunition.

The advancing Infantry made steady progress, and at 7-30 a.m. it was confirmed by the 164th Infantry Brigade that our troops were on the Knoll and were moving south. At about the same hour a message was received from the 165th Infantry Brigade, stating that the troops on the right of the Knoll attack appeared also to have taken their objective. As a matter of fact this subsequently proved not to be true, for the 1/8th Liverpools (Irish) had found the enemy wire uncut and had failed to get through. At 7-50 a.m. they were reported to be on the Knoll, but were slowly being forced back and were in need of reinforcements.

Up till now the enemy Artillery had not heavily retaliated. At Zero hour some 1,320 gas cylinders had been projected by us against the Canal Wood area, Les Tranchees, and Vendhuile. Three hundred and thirty-five Thermite bombs, together with 170 smoke bombs had also been discharged to cover the left of the 2/5th Lancashire Fusiliers. The Thermite was reported to have been very effective and to have absolutely silenced the enemy machine guns. At about 7-33 a.m., however, the enemy's Artillery became more active and a very heavy barrage came down upon our front line and continued.

No definite news had meantime been received concerning the situation at Gillemont. It was believed, however, that our troops were holding both the Knoll and Gillemont, and at 8-5 a.m. a report to that effect was received. The enemy very quickly counter-attacked. At 8-15 a.m. information was sent back to the effect that the enemy had re-entered the Knoll and that our men were falling back on Tombois.

More definite information with regard to the progress of the 1/4th King's Own Royal Lancasters was received at 8-40 a.m. Their centre company, it appeared, had met with very heavy resistance, but had gallantly succeeded in gaining the enemy trench; the left company had gone forward; of the right company no news was yet to hand. Meantime the 1/8th Liverpools (Irish) had been ordered to move northwards along the trench and to make junction with the 1/4th Royal Lancasters. The Irish, however, had, as already stated, failed to get into the enemy trenches and were re-organising in their own line.

The situation at 9 a.m. was as follows :—The 2/5th Lancashire Fusiliers had gained possession of Tiger Trench and were bombing along Tombois Trench. No news as to how far they had progressed northwards and eastwards was available, but it was reported that they had been counter-attacked. The 1/4th King's Own Royal Lancasters had taken Gillemont Switch and most of Gillemont Trench, and parties were believed to be down Loot Lane. The 1/4th King's Own Royal Lancasters were at this time using two platoons of the " Counter-attack Reserve," and at 9-20 a.m. the question of renewing the attack upon the Knoll was taken into consideration. It was decided that it was not yet time to evacuate the Knoll position and the Brigadier-General Commanding 164th Infantry Brigade was instructed to renew the attack if any chance of success offered, using, if necessary, a company of the 1/5th Liverpools, with artillery co-operation.

At 10 a.m., however, it was reported that both our battalions were off the Knoll, and orders were in consequence given that no further attack upon the Knoll should be made, and that the 1/4th King's Own Royal Lancasters should, moreover, as opportunity offered, withdraw to our original line at Gillemont. At 10-45 a.m. the Corps Commander saw the Major-General Commanding, and he expressed the wish that Gillemont should be held, at all events for the day. The Brigadier-General Commanding the 164th Infantry Brigade was instructed to that effect, and the previous order for the evacuation of Gillemont cancelled. The consolidation of the ground captured was commenced, and about noon the hostile Artillery and Trench Mortar fire became less intense, and the situation along the Divisional front appeared to be quietening down.

Not very long afterwards, however, the enemy began to show considerable activity, and succeeded in bombing our men along Gillemont Switch and in driving them back almost to No. 2 Communication Trench. The King's Own made a gallant stand and the fighting was severe, but at 1 p.m. a report was received that the left had been heavily attacked by Trench Mortars and had been bombed out of their positions, and that the right had thereupon retired to avoid the danger of being cut off. The whole Battalion, was therefore, now back on our own front line.

The enemy, all accounts agreed, had suffered very heavy casualties at Gillemont, and with the object of inflicting yet further casualties upon him, and of simulating an attack in order to keep him in doubt as to our further intentions, at 4-30 p.m. a very heavy barrage upon selected positions was put down by our Artillery, Trench Mortars and Machine Guns. It is known that this barrage caused severe casualties to the enemy. His retaliation was slight. By 4 p.m. the situation had been reported quiet all along our front, and, so far as the enemy was concerned, it remained so throughout the night. No Man's Land was patrolled by us at frequent intervals during the night, and the enemy was reported to be manifestly nervous, alert, and to be holding his line in strength. A heavy bombardment was ordered to take place upon Gillemont Farm and the Knoll at 5 a.m. next day for 10 minutes, and at 6-30 a.m. the same objectives were subjected to a hurricane bombardment for three minutes. This barrage, which contained a proportion of smoke shell, then lifted and crept forward over the enemy's support and reserve lines for 15 minutes, after which it died gradually away. The enemy expected an attack to follow and manned his trenches accordingly. No attack was, of course, intended, but once again his troops were held to their positions and prevented from proceeding northwards where the main attack was taking place.

The operation, though costly for us, was a success and achieved its object, namely, the diversion of the attention of the enemy opposite the 55th Division from the important main attack with Tanks on Cambrai, which was launched by the Third Army as a surprise on the same day. The enemy was contained, harassed, and hammered, and 26 prisoners passed through our cage. From his action against our troops it appeared highly probable that he had obtained information of our impending attack from prisoners captured during his raid at Gillemont on the night of the 18th/19th November. His front line was found to be evacuated, but his second line was strongly held, and our troops were met by a heavy rifle grenade barrage the moment they penetrated the front line trench. East of Gillemont the enemy had dug a new trench, narrow and deep, from which he fired rifle grenades. Counter-attack troops had evidently been closed up in readiness, as these troops advanced very soon after our own troops had entered his trenches. The severity of the fighting is shown by our casualties, which amounted to just over 600, killed, wounded and missing. It is known that very heavy casualties were inflicted upon the enemy.

The next few days passed quietly, although both our own and the enemy's Artillery were active. Patrols pushed out by us day and night, with constant regularity, reported the enemy to be alert and in his positions. On November 26th a good deal of movement was observed opposite our left Brigade front, and on the following day the movement was again reported to be above the normal.

During November 28th the Major-General Commanding, while making a tour of the forward area, noticed that the enemy persisted in continuous reconnaissance with low-flying aeroplanes, and that he appeared to be registering various targets with his Artillery—particularly Little Priel Farm. This farm had been consistently used by the enemy as a registration point ever since the Division arrived in the area, but on this occasion the volume of fire was so much above normal as to lead to the suspicion that many new batteries were being registered. These circumstances, added to the facts that movement behind the enemy's lines had very markedly increased, and that the enemy's Artillery was more than usually active on other targets, led the Major-General to suspect that an attack upon our front was contemplated. Upon his return to Headquarters these suspicions were communicated to the VII. Corps, to the Artillery, and to the Infantry Brigadiers. Orders were given warning all troops to be specially on the alert; special patrols were to be sent out at 4 a.m. each day to watch for enemy movement, the Field Artillery were to open fire on the enemy's front line in bursts, commencing at 5 a.m., and units in reserve were brought closer up to the line and ordered to be ready to move at half-an-hour's notice. Endeavour was also made to arrange for " counter-preparation " by Heavy Artillery on the enemy's probable assembly positions, but this vital requirement could not unfortunately be met.

In accordance with these instructions, that same afternoon the 1/4th Loyal North Lancs. from the reserve Brigade moved up to Vaucelette Farm, leaving one Company at St. Emilie, and the 2/5th Lancashire Fusiliers moved from Tincourt to Villers Faucon and occupied the billets vacated by the 1/4th Loyal North Lancs. The orders given to Lieut.-Colonel Hindle, Commanding 1/4th Loyal North Lancashire Regiment, were to counter-attack at once in case of an attack by the enemy, and to hold Villers Guislain Spur at all costs. (These orders were most loyally carried out.) Movement on the enemy's roads and back areas was again abnormal on the 29th, and positions at Villers Guislain were selected for four machine guns of the 196th Machine Gun Company, at the time in Divisional Reserve. These guns were moved into their positions that evening.

The Major-General's suspicions proved to be well-founded, and the precautionary measures taken served to prevent what might have been a very serious catastrophe. In order to explain, as clearly as possible, what took place on the morning of the 30th November, it is important to state the positions of the troops of the Division at the moment when the attack opened. And first it must be mentioned that on the 29th October the Division had taken over from the 20th Division an area of, approximately, a battalion front, thereby extending our line northwards to just beyond the Banteau Ravine —a distance of 2,500 yards. The Division was therefore now holding a frontage of 13,000 yards, supported by only two Brigades of Field Artillery ! This wide frontage could not, of course, be continuously held ; it consisted of platoon posts connected by travel trenches, and distributed in depth so far as circumstances allowed. But with such a wide front an effective distribution in depth was impossible with the troops available. On the morning of the attack the portion of the line, extending from Banteau Ravine to Wood Road, was held by the 1/5th South Lancashire Regiment. South of them in the Honnecourt sector were the 1/5th Loyal North Lancs., and in the Ossus sector the 1/10th Liverpool Scottish. The 1/5th King's Own Royal Lancasters were in support. The 165th Infantry Brigade, on the right, was disposed as follows :—1/6th Liverpools from Ossus Wood to Heythrop Post; 1/5th Liverpools from Grafton Post to Ego Post, and 1/7th Liverpools southward from this point to Cat Post and New Post. The 1/9th Liverpools were in support. The 164th Infantry Brigade were in Divisional Reserve.

THE BATTLE OF NOVEMBER 30TH.

At 7 o'clock on the morning of the 30th, in thick fog, a very heavy bombardment broke out upon the whole Divisional front, and all tracks and roads were heavily shelled. Almost simultaneously a message was received at the Headquarters of the 166th Infantry Brigade in Epehy, from the 35th Infantry Brigade, which was on our immediate left, stating that the 1/5th South Lancashire Regiment was being heavily Trench Mortared and that the S.O.S. had gone up. Communication with the Battalion was at once attempted but without result, and save for a visual signal message received at 7-43 a.m., stating : " We know nothing yet ; O.K."—nothing further was heard from the 1/5th South Lancs., nor did a man of that Battalion return.

It was presently, however, to be made clear that the enemy had broken through somewhere on the left of the 1/5th South Lancs., and was pushing forward in large numbers and with great rapidity on Villers Guislain. Between 7-38 a.m. and 7-45 a.m. Germans in considerable force were seen on Villers Ridge, and a few moments later large numbers of British troops—not of our Division—were seen to be falling back from the direction of Gonnelieu down the slopes north of the Cemetery, just north-west of Villers Guislain. Very shortly after 8 o'clock enemy machine guns were firing on our batteries from the high ground south of Gauche Wood, and enemy aeroplanes, in large numbers and flying as low as 100 feet, were subjecting Villers Guislain and the ground in its vicinity to heavy machine gun fire. At 8-15 a.m. the enemy were seen to be advancing in strong force southwards from the north of the Cemetery—*i.e.*, on the western side of Villers Guislain. The position of the village was precarious.

Meantime, as late as 7-57 a.m. the 1/5th Loyal North Lancs. had reported : " No Infantry action," but at 8-15 a.m. a message was received from the Liverpool Scottish on their right, stating that the enemy was advancing from his trenches at Ossus II. A quarter of an hour later an indistinct message from the 1/5th Loyal North Lancs. was received at the Headquarters of the 166th Infantry Brigade, to the effect that the enemy was through on the left—the line was then cut.

By 8-20 a.m. the enemy were reported to have penetrated our lines at Holt's Bank, and a few moments after large bodies of the enemy were seen in Pigeon Quarry—north of the Liverpool Scottish and between them and the 1/5th Loyal North Lancs. Almost simultaneously the enemy were reported to be coming over

in extended order and in large numbers, wave after wave, to Eagle Quarry, on the 165th Infantry Brigade front, and also to be advancing on Fleeceall Post to the south. By 9-15 a.m. the enemy had penetrated the Divisional front from the Birdcage northwards for about 800 yards, and were even reported to have been seen in Gloucester Road. Villers Guislain, turned from the north and eventually surrounded, was reported at 9-30 a.m. to be in enemy hands, and a little over half an hour later the enemy had succeeded in progressing to within a few hundred yards of Vaucelette Farm. He got no further, for he met there the 1/4th Loyal North Lancs.

The advance had been rapid and almost bewildering. Our troops, reduced in numbers, and holding, nevertheless, a front of nearly seven miles, had not merely been attacked by overwhelming numbers, but had suddenly found themselves seriously outflanked. The situation at 10-45 a.m. was undoubtedly precarious and, unless restored, might have had grave consequences. It was restored.

It is needless to say that the battalions, though sadly at a disadvantage, resisted splendidly. The 1/5th South Lancs., it was subsequently discovered, had put up a splendid fight against the troops attacking on their front, when suddenly to their amazement the enemy appeared in force *behind* them. Unable, in consequence, to replenish their stock of ammunition, they none the less fought on to the last.

The 1/5th Loyal North Lancs., placed in a very hazardous position owing to what had happened on their left, made a gallant stand and, with the Liverpool Scottish, held on at the Adelphi and

Gloucester Road, causing very severe casualties to the enemy, and very considerably delaying his advance. These troops, however, became sadly reduced in numbers and eventually, when in danger of being entirely surrounded, were compelled to withdraw, although Meath Post did not fall until 4-30 in the afternoon, and Limerick Post, garrisoned by a composite party of the 1/5th King's Own, Liverpool Scottish, and 1/5th Loyal North Lancs., though cut off and surrounded, resisted until 5 a.m. next day, when they succeeded in reaching their own lines. A magnificent counter-attack early in the morning by the 1/4th Loyal North Lancs., weak in numbers but indomitable in spirit, had not only caused the enemy very heavy losses, but had checked his advance towards Heudecourt. It was here that their gallant Commander, Lieut.-Colonel Hindle, D.S.O., fell, shot through the heart at the head of his Battalion. The North Lancs. suffered heavily, but the result of their action was that the enemy never gained a real footing on the Lempire—Epehy—Chapel-crossing Ridge. In a day of outstanding events, probably this counter-attack and subsequent stand at Vaucelette Farm is the most noteworthy, and was the most decisive in its result.

The menace to the village of Epehy, however, was serious, and it was clear that the place must, if possible, be held at all or any cost. Orders to this effect were issued by the Major-General Commanding at 10-20, and the Commander of the 166th Infantry Brigade was instructed to hang on for all he was worth, to dig in and wire, and to use all available troops for the purpose. The 1/4th King's Own Royal Lancs. were despatched from St. Emilie to Epehy to his assistance, and two sections of the 196th Machine Gun Company were also sent forward, with instructions to keep in touch with the 2/5th Lancashire Fusiliers, who had been sent to reinforce the Brigade on the right, and had already commenced to dig in from a point west of Lempire to Malassise Farm. Two Companies of the 1/4th South Lancs. (Pioneers) and the Field Company R.E. from Divisional Reserve, were sent to occupy posts on the line Malassise Farm (inclusive) to the northern end of Peziere, and the 4th and 5th Cavalry Divisions were ordered up, and shortly after noon were reported to be approaching Roisel. A battalion of the 24th Division (13th Middlesex) was ordered to move up to St. Emilie, and a second battalion was ordered up to strengthen Lempire and Ronssoy. These two battalions were placed at the disposal of G.O.C. 55th Division. The importance of holding on to Lempire was impressed upon all units concerned, and arrangements were made for further reinforcements of men and of guns for the defence of the village should a serious attack be made upon it. Labour Companies and all other available troops were collected and disposed for the defence of the villages, and by 12-30 p.m. all the troops of the 55th Division were engaged.

The situation on the right by this time was considerably easier. By 9-50 a.m. the 1/5th Liverpools had been able to telegraph that the attack upon their front was contained and had been driven back. The attack further south, upon the front of the 1/7th Liverpools, had made no progress. The 1/6th Liverpools, their line penetrated, were, none the less, holding on magnificently; Cruciform Post and Heythrop Farm remained in our possession, and Little Priel Farm—lost for a few moments only—had been re-taken. The Brigade had been reinforced at 9-30 a.m. by the 2/5th Lancashire Fusiliers, who had been ordered to dig in from Lempire to Malassise Farm. This line was actually completed by 1-25 p.m. —a very smart and valuable piece of work. The 1/9th Liverpools, in Brigade support, were distributed on the right of the Lancashire Fusiliers with one Company in the posts at Zebra, Yak, Lempire Central, and Lempire East, and one Company reinforcing the 1/6th Liverpools in Little Priel Cutting.

The position, therefore, at mid-day was something as follows :—The line of the 165th Infantry Brigade was intact as far as Grafton Post from the south. From Grafton Post the line ran to Heythrop Post, Little Priel Farm and Cruciform Post. Kildare Post was in possession of the enemy, but Meath Post and Limerick Post were still holding out. The position north and west was obscure, but Vaucelette Farm, Epehy, Malassise Farm and May Copse were in our possession. North of this line there did not seem to be any troops, and we had ceased to be in touch with the Division on our left. At 1-25 p.m. the 1/8th Liverpool Irish and the 13th Middlesex, were thereupon ordered to move to a point north of Peziere, and the former were ordered to push posts forward between Peziere and Vaucelette Farm, extending the left of the 166th Brigade, and to get into touch with the 1/4th Loyal North Lancs., who were still gallantly holding Vaucelette Farm. The 13th Middlesex were ordered to hold from Vaucelette Farm northwards to Chapel Hill and to maintain touch with the Division on the left. The line Epehy—Vaucelette Farm—Chapel Hill Crossing was to be held at all costs. The Brigadier-General Commanding 164th Infantry Brigade was placed in command of this section of the front at 1-15 p.m., and in addition to the three battalions above mentioned, had at his disposal eight machine guns of the 164th Machine Gun Company.

The afternoon passed without serious incident, although the heavy fighting continued and the situation remained tense and anxious. All ranks were, however, determined to fight to the last and not to give up one inch of ground. About 3 p.m. the enemy heavily shelled Heythrop and Cruciform Posts, and a large body of Germans were reported to be advancing along Catelet Valley. These were dealt with by our Artillery. The enemy was also reported to be massing, under cover of his own machine guns, in Parr's Bank, and shortly after 3 o'clock another attack was made on Grafton Post and Little Priel Farm, but was effectively repulsed. At 3-40 p.m. orders were sent out to all as follows :—

" Following line will be consolidated and held at all costs :—165th Infantry Brigade from Basse Boulogne South to Malassise Farm inclusive. 166th Infantry Brigade from latter point through X. 26. central to high ground about X. 25. b. 164th Infantry Brigade from latter point to Vaucelette Farm, special attention to be paid to north flank. Any posts or trenches east of the above line to be held to the last. 165th Infantry Brigade will report if they can withdraw any troops for use further north."

The north flank was still the anxiety. The 165th Brigade was, however, unable to despatch any troops to strengthen it. Two companies of the 2nd Queen's (West Surreys) had begun to arrive to support this Brigade at 4-45 p.m., but they were urgently required for the Little Priel Farm area, where an intense struggle continued. As a matter of fact, their support proved not to be required upon the north flank. The line was held, and at 7 p.m. the situation was reported to be substantially the same as in the early afternoon, and can be discerned from the map. This situation remained practically unaltered until the relief of the Division the day but one following. The attack had been held and checked.

At midnight the information was communicated to all concerned that at 6-30 next morning (December 1st) two parties of Tanks were to attack eastwards—one party north of Chapel Hill towards Gauche Wood and one party north of Vaucelette Farm towards Villers Guislain. One Cavalry Brigade was to attack Gauche Wood and another Villers Guislain; the Cavalry Corps was to advance in the direction of the high ground about Villers Hill and Villers Ridge; and at the same time the Guards Division was to attack in the direction of Gonnelieu. The 164th and 166th Infantry Brigades were ordered to keep close touch with this advance and to take every opportunity to advance their line in conjunction with the Cavalry on their left. They were instructed, however, only to advance if the Cavalry were known to have reached and to have secured an objective. The 164th Brigade was ordered to keep both the 165th and 166th Brigades informed of the progress of the Cavalry advance.

The attack was launched as projected, but met with scant success. The Cavalry, after suffering heavy casualties, succeeded in occupying the southern portion of Kildare Post, and a little progress was made in the direction of Villers Guislain, but generally the line remained unchanged. During the night December 1st

2nd the 164th and 166th Brigades were relieved by the 21st Division, who took over the front from Malassise Farm to Vaucelette Farm—both farms exclusive. The Division, therefore, now held a Brigade front only. Desultory fighting on the whole front continued without intermission during the succeeding days.

On the 6th and 7th December the Division was relieved by the 16th Division and moved into the Flamicourt area prior to proceeding north for a well-earned and much needed rest. The men, as the newspaper account subsequently stated, "had fought like tigers." "*By sheer stubbornness and the most heroic resistance, a mere handful of British troops on our right checked the Hun avalanche until our supports could arrive.*" . . . . "*It was glorious fighting, which must have earned even the enemy's utmost respect.*"

The Division had distinguished itself at Ypres on July 31st and on September 20th, and had earned and received the praise of the high authorities. Battered and weakened, it had taken over this ill-defended 13,000 yards of frontage south of Cambrai. Battered again in the attack of November 20th, with one Brigade (164th) more than decimated, it had been called upon to withstand the main shock of the most severe and the most serious attack the enemy had made since the 2nd Battle of Ypres in the Spring of 1915. The 55th Division has had proud days in the course of its history, but none prouder than November 30th, 1917. Only two of our men passed through the straggler posts.

On leaving the area the following message was received from Lieut.-General Sir T. D'O. Snow, K.C.B., K.C.M.G., Commanding VII. Corps :—

" The Corps Commander cannot allow the 55th Division to leave his command without expressing to the Officers, non-commissioned officers and men, his satisfaction at the way they fought and worked during the recent operations.

" It is not at present quite clear what happened on the left of the Division, but, from the enquiries made by the Corps Commander, he knows that the 30th November, 1917, in spite of the heavy losses incurred, was a day which will always reflect credit on the 55th Division.

" The fact that not a man returned from the 1/5th South Lancs. Regiment, when that battalion was attacked by overwhelming numbers, tells its own tale.

" He wishes the Division, and his old friend, its Commander, the best of luck.

                (*Signed*) J. BURNETT STUART,
                                  Brigadier-General.
8/12/17.   General Staff, VII. Corps."

CHAPTER V.

GIVENCHY—FESTUBERT.

The Division was now transferred to the First Army and, with the exception of the Artillery, arrived in the Bomy area—near Fruges—for training on the 14th December. The Artillery were retained in their positions in the line after the other units had left, and did not arrive in the Bomy Artillery area until the 4th of January. On December 31st the Pioneer Battalion and the 422nd Field Company R.E. were moved up to the Givenchy—Festubert area for the purpose of strengthening the defences there in view of a probable hostile attack, and on the 8th January the 276th Brigade R.F.A. were ordered forward to Robecq. Training meantime was vigorously proceeded with, and especial attention was given to musketry. On the 20th January the 419th Field Company R.E. moved to Hinges, and on the 24th the 423rd Field Company R.E. relieved the 422nd Field Company R.E. at Le Preol.

For some little time past rumour had hinted that a reduction of the establishment of Divisions was in contemplation, and on the 14th January notification was received from the I. Corps that the number of battalions per Division was henceforth to be reduced to nine, excluding the Pioneer Battalion. A week later an order was received directing three battalions to proceed to the 57th Division for amalgamation with second line units. This order was received with great regret throughout the Division, though the reason for it was, of course, obvious. The battalions detailed to proceed were the 1/8th Liverpool Irish, the 1/9th Liverpools and the 1/5th Loyal North Lancs., and these units left the Division to join the 57th on the 31st of January. Everyone was sorry to see them go and the Major-General expressed the general sentiment of the Division in the following :—

"55th (West Lancashire) Division.

"SPECIAL ORDER OF THE DAY.

"31st January, 1918.

"On the departure from the Division of three battalions—the 1/8th The King's Liverpool Regt. (Liverpool Irish), 1/9th The King's Liverpool Regt., and 1/5th Loyal North Lancashire Regt.—I wish to assure all officers, warrant officers, non-commissioned officers and men belonging to them, how greatly I, and, I am sure, everyone in the Division, regrets their loss.

"Some, I am glad to say, remain with us.

"As to the Battalions themselves, I refuse to regard the separation as permanent, and I look forward confidently to the day when they will rejoin their old Division.

"They have had their full share in all the hard fighting of the past two years, and have helped to make and maintain the reputation which the Division has gained—a reputation which, I am sure, makes every member of it proud of belonging to it. As for myself, to have commanded it during these years is the highest privilege.

"I hope that eventually the Liverpool Irish the 9th King's, and the 5th Loyal North Lancs. may rejoin our ranks, and that the final blow may be given shoulder to shoulder with them.

" Till they come back again I wish them, on the part of the Division and myself, all good fortune and success, and can assure them that we shall watch their career as keenly as if they were still with us.

"H. S. JEUDWINE,
"Major-General,
"Commanding 55th Division."

This letter was very keenly appreciated by all ranks. Unfortunately the General's hope was not realised. The three battalions never came back to us in the Field, but they sustained their reputation in the ranks of our sister Division in the heavy fighting in which that Division was subsequently engaged.

The Division received its orders to move forward on the 4th February, and at 10 a.m. on the 15th, the Division relieved the 42nd (East Lancashire) Division on the left sector of the I. Corps front. The portion of the line taken over extended northwards from beyond the La Bassee—Cambrin Road to Cailloux Road, northeast of Festubert; but on March 5th the portion of the Divisional area south of the La Bassee Canal was taken over by the 46th Division.

The first spell of fighting took place on February 17th, when, at about 3-15 a.m., a party of the enemy, about 30 strong, rushed our post at Warlingham Crater. The enemy was, however, promptly turned out and pursued back to his own lines, suffering casualties. After this things remained fairly quiet until the 7th March, when the enemy heavily raided the 1/5th South Lancs., but was driven off after having caused us 43 casualties.

At midnight on the 6th/7th the orders for the formation of the 55th Battalion Machine Gun Corps came into force. This Battalion was composed of the 164th, 165th, 166th and 196th Machine Gun Companies, which henceforward were designated A, B, C and D Companies respectively.

About this time information was received to the effect that the enemy was very considerably strengthening his artillery on our Corps front and that several Austrian batteries had recently arrived. It was also known, not only that many new trench mortars had been built in, but that their numbers were daily being increased. Precautions were thereupon taken to reinforce the line held by the Portuguese on our immediate left, if—as seemed not unlikely—an attack upon the front held by our Allies were to take place. The necessary orders to ensure this reinforcement were issued on the 13th March, and the task was deputed to the Brigade in Divisional Reserve.

On March 18th at 5 a.m. a raid was carried out by the 1/5th King's Own, and the enemy's lines were entered at three points. The raiding party, which consisted of a Company of Infantry and one N.C.O. and six Sappers R.E., penetrated both the front and support trenches of the enemy, but no Germans were seen. A further raid by the same battalion took place just after midnight on the 25th March, and the raiding party succeeded in penetrating as far as the enemy reserve line, capturing nine prisoners and a machine gun at the cost of but a few, slightly wounded, casualties. Our artillery barrage on this occasion was even more than usually effective and came in for a special tribute from the raiders.

The southern boundary of the Division was extended on the 27th March, and a portion of the line south of the La Bassee Canal was again taken over by the Division—the 166th Infantry Brigade relieving a Brigade of the 46th Division. Our tenure of this line was, however, destined to be a very short one, for on the night of the 6th/7th April the 166th Infantry Brigade was relieved by a Brigade of the 1st Division and went into Divisional Reserve. This relief was momentous and had far-reaching consequences, as will presently be seen.

The early days of April were quiet and uneventful, though it was generally recognised that the quiet was but the prelude of a coming storm. For this storm, whenever it came, our preparations had been made and the necessary dispositions formulated. The Artillery continued their programme of wire-cutting and of shelling all movement and working parties in and behind the enemy lines, and at 1 a.m. on the 6th of April 500 gas drums were fired from projectors against the enemy's trenches. Patrols sent out each night, at irregular periods, for four hours each, penetrated as far as the enemy support lines without encountering opposition, and even on the night 8th/9th of April a patrol which was out on our front from 10 p.m. to 2 a.m. found the enemy trenches unoccupied.

The 166th Infantry Brigade was in the Beuvry—Le Preol area on the 8th April in Divisional Reserve, as has been stated. The enemy had counted on this, and, in an order captured from him, had boasted that it would be prevented by his powerful artillery fire from taking part in the fight for Festubert and Givenchy. Reasons, however, supervened which made it advisable to relieve the right Brigade of the 2nd Portuguese

Division on our immediate left, and the 166th Infantry Brigade was, on the afternoon of the 8th, brought from the Le Preol area to the Locon area to be ready to relieve the Portuguese next day—the 9th. By 5 p.m., therefore, on the 8th April, the 166th Infantry Brigade was disposed as follows :—Headquarters and the Brigade Signal Section in Locon ; 1/5th King's Own Royal Lancasters in and about Locon ; 1/10th Liverpool Scottish at Mesplaux Farm and Le Hamel ; 1/5th South Lancs. at Le Hamel and Essars, with the Light Trench Mortar Battery in Locon. At 9 p.m. the Portuguese Commander with his Staff arrived in Locon to arrange the details of the relief of his Brigade, and everything was in order for the relief to take place the following day. It did not take place for reasons which will now appear.

At 4 o'clock on the morning of the 9th April the dispositions of the Division were as follows :—The 164th Infantry Brigade on the right was holding the line from the La Bassee Canal to the north of Givenchy. 1/4th King's Own Royal Lancasters held the right of this line and the 1/4th Loyal North Lancs. held the left. The 2/5th Lancashire Fusiliers were in support at Gorre, with two companies at Windy Corner. The 165th Infantry Brigade on the left was holding from the north of Givenchy to the left boundary—including Festubert—employing the 1/7th Liverpools on the right and the 1/5th Liverpools on the left, with the 1/6th Liverpools in support—one company behind Festubert with the 1/7th King's Liverpools, and one company behind Le Plantin, supporting the 1/5th King's Liverpools ; two companies of the 1/6th were in Gorre. The 166th Infantry Brigade was in reserve. All Infantry in the line were told off definitely to one of two tasks, either as

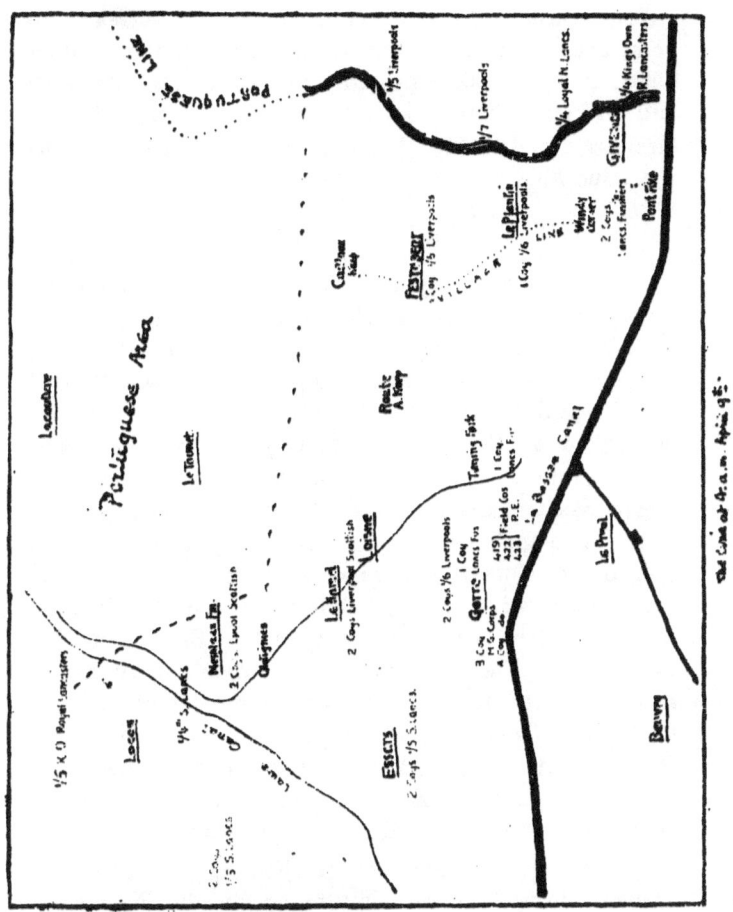

garrisons—whose duty it was to hold their posts to the last, no matter whether outflanked or surrounded—or as counter-attack troops, for immediate local counter-attack. Their action in different situations had been practised by means of tactical exercises. The preliminary battle positions of the Reserve Brigade, to be taken up on attack becoming imminent, had been laid down beforehand, and practised repeatedly in tactical exercises with and without troops. To put the Reserve Brigade and all other details in the Division into their battle positions the issue of a code word only was necessary.

THE BATTLE OF APRIL 9TH, 1918.

It was about 4-15 a.m. that a very heavy bombardment opened on the whole Divisional front, and, in addition, every village in the back area, all roads, crossings, tracks and canal bridges as far back as, and even beyond, Locon, were severely shelled. The morning was raw and cold and a heavy mist lay over the whole area. Prompt with the bombardment the reserve troops received the code word " Bustle," and proceeded to move to their battle positions shortly after 4-30 a.m. The bombardment considerably slackened about 6-30 a.m., and it was then reported that it had merely indicated a raid on a large scale upon two Brigades of the Portuguese. The 165th Infantry Brigade were, nevertheless, ordered to get into touch immediately with the Portuguese Brigade and to report what had happened. It afterwards transpired that a serious attack had been made and pushed home, but throughout the day no information was received from the Portuguese.

At 8 o'clock, or thereabouts, the bombardment again opened out and almost simultaneously the Portuguese on our left were forced back from their trenches, and before 9 o'clock the whole of our left flank was exposed. The infantry attack upon our Divisional front commenced at about 9 o'clock. The heavy mist—visibility was limited to between 20 and 30 yards—enabled the enemy to get close up to our positions before being exposed to really effective fire. As a consequence he succeeded, on the 164th Infantry Brigade front, in penetrating the front line, and was actually attacking the Battalion Headquarters of the 1/4th Loyal North Lancs. by 9-30 a.m. Moat Farm was surrounded and the ruins of Givenchy Church occupied by the enemy, though the garrisons in both places were holding on. South of Givenchy the Germans penetrated as far as Gunner Siding on the Cuinchy—Givenchy Road, and Death-and-Glory Sap was cut off, but held out and was never taken. On the extreme left of the 164th Infantry Brigade the enemy had broken through to Le Plantin South; had penetrated beyond the Pont Fixe—Festubert Road at the point of junction with the 165th Brigade; had occupied some houses at Windy Corner, and had even succeeded in pushing a patrol or two as far as Lone Farm.

Counter measures were immediately taken and the situation was soon restored. The tenacity of the garrisons who held on—though in many places surrounded—and pinned the enemy to the ground, prevented the attack from being further developed, and local counter-attacks, conducted with splendid initiative and energy by Company, Platoon and Section Commanders on the spot, soon resulted in the re-capture of all the ground occupied, together with a large number of prisoners and machine guns. By the early afternoon the situation on the front of this Brigade had been completely restored and the Brigade held all its original line, with the exception of a few of the forward posts and saps. These were re-occupied about dusk without great opposition, and at the end of the day this Brigade held every inch of its original ground.

Meantime what had been happening on the 165th Infantry Brigade front ? Shortly after 8-30 a.m. the old British line had been heavily attacked and its flank turned by the Germans, who, in consequence of the Portuguese retirement, had been able to advance from the north and *behind* the garrison. By 9-50 a.m. the Village Line along the Pont Fixe—Festubert Road (the main line of resistance) was attacked, although parts of the old British line were still holding out gallantly, and other posts in front of it continued to hold out for a considerable period after this. It was, indeed, owing to the determined fighting of the garrisons of these advanced posts that the attack was considerably broken up and disorganised, and only succeeded in penetrating the main defences on the extreme right of the Brigade. In this neighbourhood the enemy had occupied Windy Corner and had attacked Le Plantin South from the right and from the rear. The latter post, indeed, was occupied, but a determined local attack soon completely restored the situation, and captured numerous prisoners and machine guns. Although the attack was pushed, again and again, with extreme determination, at no other point was the line penetrated.

But the extreme left was causing much anxiety owing to the retirement of the Portuguese. Left entirely in the air, and exposed to attack from the north and from the west, the situation demanded serious attention. Route A Keep, an important post—subsequently to become famous—was captured at 11 a.m. by the enemy, who had been able to approach it, under cover of thick fog, from the rear, and shortly after noon the Brigadier-

General Commanding the 165th Infantry Brigade, whose Headquarters were in Loisne Chateau, reported that the enemy could be seen moving across in front of Loisne Central, and that his Headquarters were under machine gun fire from both flanks.

As soon as the threat to the left flank became known a defensive flank was thrown back by support troops of the 165th Infantry Brigade from Cailloux Keep through the northern extremity of the Tuning Fork Locality to Loisne Central Keep. The Headquarters and two companies of the 1/6th Liverpools had been ordered forward as early as 4-30 a.m., and under a very heavy barrage had taken up position in the Tuning Fork line with one platoon in Route A Keep. Soon after 7 a.m. the Liverpool Scottish, from the 166th Infantry Brigade, had also arrived in the Tuning Fork Locality and were disposed with one company in the Switch and three companies in the Tuning Fork Line to Loisne Central. This battalion was placed under the orders of the Brigadier-General Commanding the 165th Infantry Brigade at 12 noon.

The two remaining companies of the 1/6th Liverpools had been sent to reinforce the 1/5th and 1/7th Liverpools in the Village Line at 9-45 a.m., and at 1-20 p.m. all spare men from the units came up from the transport lines and were formed into a company and placed along the banks of the stream to defend the left rear of the Brigade Headquarters. At 2 p.m. two companies of the 1/5th South Lancs. from the Reserve Brigade were also placed under the orders of the 165th Infantry Brigade, and were placed in positions north of Loisne to repel an attack from the north. Attempt after attempt was made during the afternoon by the enemy to penetrate this defensive flank, and desperate fighting took place. The line held firm, however, and was, in fact, never afterwards broken.

The 166th Infantry Brigade had received its orders to move up into its battle positions at 4-30 a.m., and was in process of so doing, when, at 6-35 a.m.—in consequence of the report from the 2nd Portuguese Division that the heavy bombardment had merely indicated a strong hostile raid on their positions and that the bombardment was subsiding—the Major-General ordered the Brigadier-General Commanding to halt his Brigade. This order was, however, very shortly afterwards cancelled and the Brigade proceeded to its battle positions. The development of the action soon necessitated the detachment of two battalions—the Liverpool Scottish and two companies of the 1/5th South Lancs. being placed under the orders of the 165th Infantry Brigade, as stated, and the other two companies of the 1/5th South Lancs. were despatched to the assistance of the 164th Infantry Brigade. The remaining battalion, the 1/5th King's Own Royal Lancasters, had set out to take up the position detailed to it—Le Touret to Loisne Central—and in spite of the heavy mist and the severe barrage had occupied most of their positions by the early afternoon. The importance of the occupation of the Le Touret line was very early seen to be of the most extreme urgency, and the 1/5th King's Own had been instructed that this line must be reached and held, whatever happened and whatever the cost.

Meantime, orders had already been given for the 1/4th South Lancs. (Pioneers) and the 419th, 422nd and 423rd Field Companies R.E. to reinforce the 166th Infantry Brigade and at about 1 p.m. the Pioneers and

Photo by Mendoza, London, W.

Brig.-General T. E. TOPPING, C.B., C.M.G., D.S.O., T.D.
276th Brigade R.F.A.

Lt.-Col. J. J. SHUTE, C.M.G., D.S.O., T.D.
1/5th King's (L'pool Regt.)

Photo by Bacon & Sons, Liverpool

Lt.-Col. J. B. McKAIG, D.S.O.
1/6th King's (L'pool Regt.)

Photo by Kay, Bolton

Lt.-Col. C. K. POTTER, D.S.O., M.C.
1/5th Loyal North Lancs. Regt.
Commanding 1/7th King's (L'pool Regt.)

Photo by Romney Studios, Ltd.

Major H. K. S. WOODHOUSE, D.S.O.
1/5th King's (L'pool Regt.)
Commanding 1/9th King's (L'pool Regt.)

the 419th and 423rd Field Companies had arrived at Mesplaux Farm from Gorre Wood, and came under the orders of the Brigadier-General Commanding the 166th Infantry Brigade. A detachment of the 251st Tunnelling Company was also ordered up to the Mesplaux Farm area for the strengthening of the defensive flank.

Early in the morning the 154th Brigade of the 51st Division, which was at the time in the Busnes area, was ordered forward and placed under the orders of the G.O.C. 55th Division. Of this Brigade a battalion —the 1/4th Seaforth Highlanders—was placed at the disposal of the 166th Infantry Brigade; the remainder of the Brigade (154th) was used to cover Locon and Les Caudrons from the north. The Officer Commanding the Seaforths arrived to report at the 166th Brigade Headquarters at 2 p.m., and was instructed to move his battalion forthwith to Mesplaux Farm and await orders. At 2-45 p.m. the 422nd Field Company R.E., together with a party of about 50 Infantry, arrived, and at once received orders to occupy the portion of the flank extending down to the Lawe Canal.

It was shortly after this time that the 1/5th King's Own reported that the enemy was working round to the North and that he was already in possession of Le Touret Village. Immediately upon receipt of this intelligence the 1/4th Seaforths were ordered to advance from Mesplaux Farm to fill up the gap which existed between the King's Own and the Pioneers, and to get in touch as soon as possible with both these units. By 5 o'clock the Officer Commanding the Seaforths was able to report that he was in position and that he believed himself to be in touch with both flanks.

Severe fighting took place during the rest of the day, especially round Mesplaux Farm, and the enemy made numerous and determined efforts to break through. But the line held, and evening saw the defensive flank complete and firm, and the enemy definitely opposed by two lines of defence, with a third (Gorre—Le Hamel—Lawe River) in course of formation.

The close of the day's fighting, therefore, found the Division, with the assistance of the 154th Infantry Brigade, holding a front of about 11,000 yards—from the La Bassee Canal to the west of the Lawe Canal 2,000 yards north-east of Locon, whence it was prolonged —though not continuously—by troops of the 51st Division. Practically every rifle in the Division had been put into the line, and all details used as Infantry. The right Brigade—164th—held the whole of its original line intact; the left Brigade—165th—held the whole of its line of resistance and had, in addition, thrown back a flank at right angles for some 2,000 yards. Both Brigades had, moreover, a very substantial haul of prisoners.

At 5 p.m. Divisional Headquarters, which was by then in unsuitable proximity to the front line, was moved to Hinges Chateau, under arrangements made in view of such a contingency.

In several instances the enemy had approached to within 200 yards of guns in action. In some cases these were pulled out of their pits and used point blank, doing fine execution. In other cases the battery rifles and Lewis Guns were called into play, and took equally satisfactory toll of the enemy. In no single instance did the enemy get into a battery position. An anti-tank gun of the 276th Brigade, in the open on Givenchy Hill

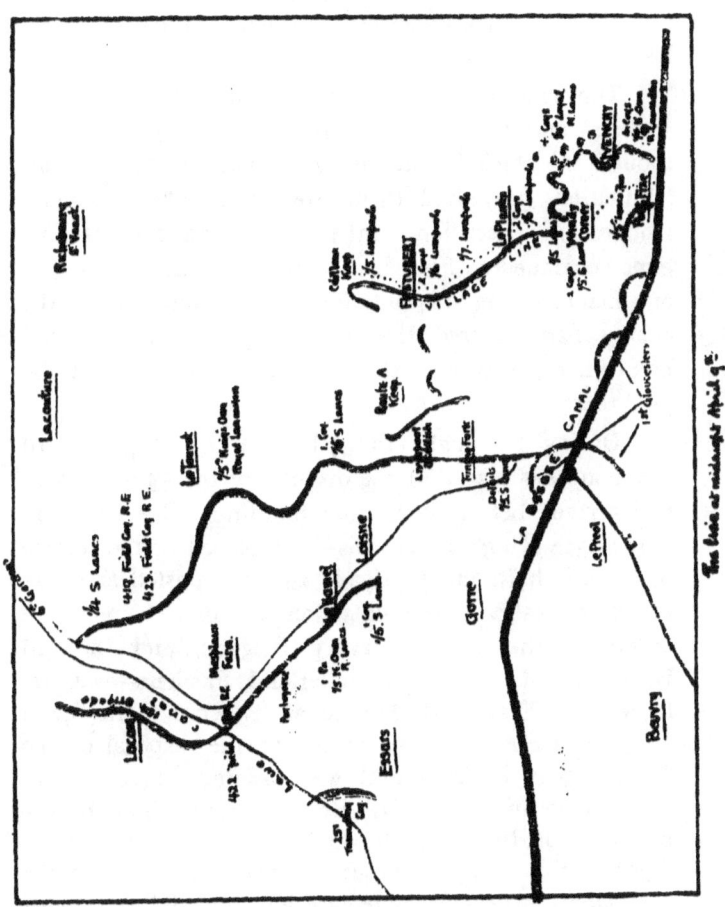

and within 500 yards of the front line, though surrounded and damaged by enemy fire, continued firing at point blank range throughout the action. Several six inch trench mortars in the same locality, after firing until the enemy was on top of them, also used their rifles with great effect. As a result no guns or trench mortars were lost.

Throughout the heavy fighting on all fronts, rifles Vickers' and Lewis Guns were used with great effect, though the thick fog in the earlier part of the day unfortunately prevented them from doing the maximum amount of execution. In several instances machine guns continued to fire when completely surrounded, and one machine gun was actually kept in action after the enemy had entered the rear compartment of a pill box, where he was checked by the revolver fire of the gun team.

During the night the 9th Infantry Brigade (3rd Division) was placed at the disposal of the 55th Division and arrived before dawn next morning. One battalion —the 13th King's Liverpools—was placed at the service of the 165th Infantry Brigade and was posted at Gorre to act as reserve; one battalion was placed under the orders of the 164th Infantry Brigade, and the 3rd Battalion—the 1st Northumberland Fusiliers—was retained in Essars as Divisional Reserve. The 42nd Brigade R.F.A. was also placed at the disposal of the C.R.A. 55th Division and was ordered to come into action covering the 166th Brigade front. Two of the batteries of this Brigade, however, were detached at 8-30 next morning in order to cover the front of the 51st Division on our immediate left, and did not revert to the 55th Division until the morning of the 11th. The arrival of this artillery group at dawn on the 10th was a great source of relief to the Brigadier-General Commanding the 166th Brigade, and rendered most efficient service.

At 7-40 on the morning of the 10th the enemy fiercely resumed his attacks upon Loisne, advancing in large numbers from the north under an extremely heavy barrage. A company of the 1/5th South Lancs. was thereupon sent to reinforce Loisne Central, and severe fighting took place. Our men, however, refused to give ground, and after many attempts to penetrate our line, and having suffered very heavy casualties, the enemy was beaten off at 9-30. A heavy attack was also made upon " B " company of the 1/5th King's Own about 8-20 a.m. at Le Touret, and was strongly pressed. This attack was accompanied by a bombardment of the whole front of the 166th Brigade and of the back areas. The attempt, however, failed, and once again heavy casualties were sustained by the enemy. Determined, however, to break through our defensive flank, yet another attack—as fierce as its predecessor—was launched at 1 p.m. against " B " company 1/5th King's Own, and this time succeeded in compelling the company to withdraw a distance of 200 yards. This withdrawal only took place after a very gallant fight, in which the company lost 100 men out of a total strength of 140, and a counter-attack by the 1/5th King's Own at 2-20 p.m. completely restored the situation and drove the enemy back to his own line. In the early afternoon a strong battalion—the 1st Northumberland Fusiliers—was placed under the orders of the 166th Brigade, and the defence of this flank was believed to be secure; which, indeed, proved to be the case.

Baffled in his attempts to force us back at Le Touret, the enemy, at 7 o'clock in the evening, launched a second violent attack upon our battered positions at Loisne, and so severely was the attack pressed that he succeeded in gaining a temporary footing in our line. His success, however, was short lived, and he was hurled back once more to his own lines, this time leaving 21 prisoners and two machine guns in our hands. We were not further disturbed that night.

It was obvious, however, that the enemy must make yet a further attempt to break the serried line which threatened seriously to discount his successes further north, and which baffled his hopes of becoming master of Bethune and of the rich coal mining district surrounding it. Great importance, manifestly, attached to the possession of Bethune, and it was known that the enemy meant to have it at any cost. He did not get it ; but, it must be admitted, he tried his best for it.

At 7 o'clock on the evening of the 10th the Major-General ordered the 165th Infantry Brigade to move their Headquarters from Loisne Chateau to the Ferme du Roi, near Bethune, and this was done next morning. Meantime, the Village Line was subjected to a terrific bombardment with shells of heavy calibre, and the defences were practically obliterated by the bombardment. All posts were, however, held intact, and all were ready to hold on still, whatever happened.

At daybreak on the 11th the shelling of our front, support and reserve lines was resumed, and the back areas again came in for attention. This shelling grew into a bombardment shortly before 8 o'clock and continued with great intensity until 11 o'clock, when an attack was launched from Loisne to the Lawe Canal, and the centre and left of the 166th Infantry Brigade were slightly pressed back. For a time a distinctly dangerous gap was made in our line, but a spirited counter-attack by the 1/4th South Lancs. from Mesplaux Farm, and the 1st Northumberland Fusiliers from Les Facons, restored the situation at a critical moment and the danger passed.

In the early afternoon the enemy was reported to be advancing in great strength between Rue Cailloux and Quinque Rue, and was, moreover, reported to be massing all along the old British line. The artillery were promptly informed and were turned on to this concentration, inflicting such heavy casualties upon the enemy that the attack upon the southern portion of the front of the 165th Infantry Brigade was never able to develop. More to the north, however, the attack was pressed home, and, after a stiff fight, and with heavy losses, the enemy succeeded in capturing Festubert East and Cailloux Keep shortly after 4 p.m. Counter-attacks were immediately ordered and Festubert East was re-captured without much difficulty. A stiffer resistance was expected from Cailloux and two counter-attacks were prepared against it—the first to be delivered by troops in the Festubert locality, and, in case of failure, a second, on a considerably larger scale, by troops from the Brigade Reserve. The first attack, however, did not fail, and by 7-30 p.m. Cailloux Keep was in our possession once more and the whole of the line completely restored.

In the course of the night of April 11th certain reliefs and re-arrangements took place on the 165th Infantry Brigade front, and arrangements were made for the artillery of the 164th Infantry Brigade to register on Route A Keep the following day. The re-capture of this Keep was of immense importance and would considerably strengthen our left flank. It was decided,

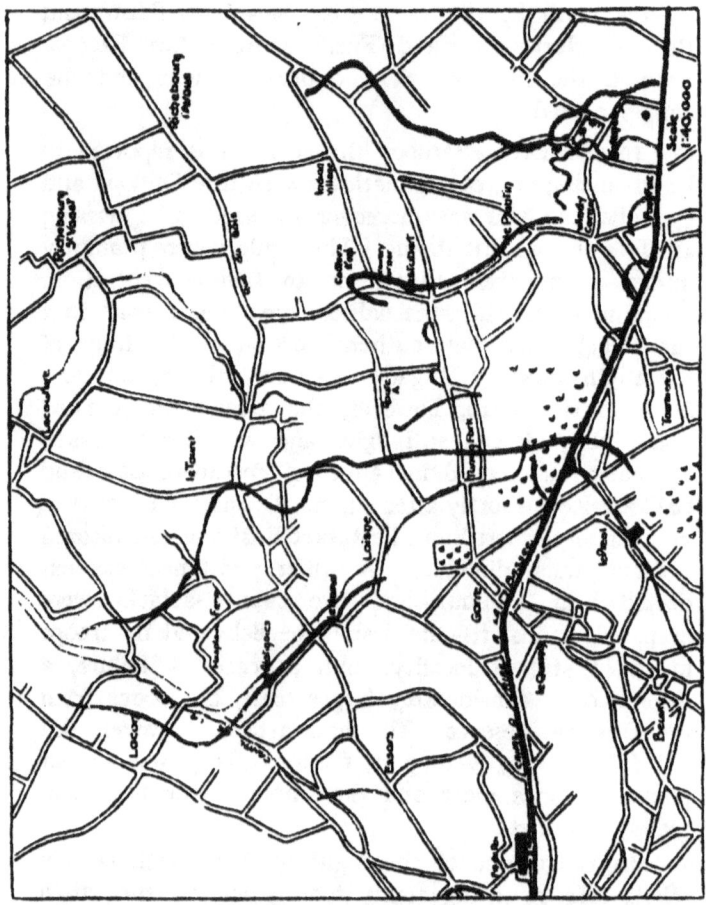

therefore, that an attempt should be made at midnight on the 12th, and trench mortars were sent up during the day and also registered on the Keep. The attack was entrusted to a company of the Liverpool Scottish and a company of the 13th Liverpools, and promptly at midnight these troops advanced under the artillery and trench mortar barrage, and after a stiff fight—for the Germans, as well as ourselves, realised the importance of the position, and were determined to retain it at any cost—we captured the Keep. A strong counter-attack at dawn next morning was repulsed. A further attack at 5-30 in the afternoon was launched against the Keep, and very severe fighting again took place for its possession. But we were determined to hold what we had won, and though we suffered heavy casualties the end of the fight saw the Keep still in our possession, and it remained in our possession during the rest of our tenure of the line until our relief.

After the re-capture of Route A Keep no further German attacks of serious importance were attempted. Our lines, cross roads, bridges, and back areas were kept under heavy shell fire, and our troops were kept continuously upon the alert. But the line remained firm, and on April 14th the relief of the Division commenced. The 166th Infantry Brigade was relieved on the night of the 14th/15th, the 165th Infantry Brigade on the 15th/16th, and the 164th Infantry Brigade on the 16th/17th; the artillery remained in the line; the rest of the Division went back to the Auchel area. The line held by the 55th Division now passed to the 1st and 3rd Divisions, the former taking over the right and centre of our old front and the latter the left.

So ended the battle of Givenchy—Festubert. It had been in many ways a replica of the battle for Epehy on the 30th November, 1917. Once again we had been called upon to fight with our flank in the air; once again it had been ours to throw out and maintain a thin defensive flank against an enemy flushed with success and in almost overwhelming force; once again we were placed in a position where to give ground meant the possible sacrifice of the whole front, with consequences of almost catastrophic calamity—and once again we held on. The portion of the line held by the Division from February to September, 1918, was the only section of the whole Allied front, which, being attacked in force, during the great German offensive, was held to the end inviolate. And it was afterwards publicly stated by an Officer of the German General Staff that the stand made by the Division on April 9th and the days which followed marked the final ruination of the supreme German effort of 1918.

As a result of the operation our captures amounted to nearly 1,000 prisoners and 70 machine guns. Our casualties were necessarily heavy, and amounted to 163 Officers and 2,956 other ranks, killed, wounded and missing. That the enemy's casualties were enormous we have good reason to know—we passed through his cemeteries during our advance in October and we saw for ourselves.

The following Special Order of the Day was subsequently issued to all ranks :—

SPECIAL ORDER OF THE DAY.

To all ranks of

The 55th (West Lancashire) Division.

"Now that the hard and anxious struggle of the last eight days has come to an end, I want to thank and congratulate the whole Division and tell you how proud I am of the magnificent fighting spirit you have shown. To have defended against determined and continuous attack the line originally entrusted to you, and to have held in addition against an incessant pressure an extended flank thrown back for several thousand yards when the enemy broke through on your left, is an achievement worthy of the best traditions of the British Army.

"The result has been due to the foresight and dogged determination of Brigadiers and all Commanders, and of the troops under them, and to the resolution and self-sacrifice of all arms and all ranks.

"The situation of the British Army is still critical, and must remain so until the enemy's strength has been worn down and broken. We have still much hard work and fighting in front of us before an honourable and satisfactory peace can be assured. Our present duty, as soon as all ranks are rested, is to fit ourselves in every possible way to meet the enemy again, and to prepare to teach him another lesson. If only this preparation is undertaken by the 55th Division in the same spirit of grim determination that it has shown in action, I have no fear of the result.

"H. S. JEUDWINE,
"Major-General,
"Commanding 55th (West Lancashire)
17th April, 1918." "Division.

The Special Supplementary Despatch, together with an extract from General Despatch of the Commander-in-Chief, are printed below :—

SPECIAL SUPPLEMENTARY DESPATCH.

"THE 55TH DIVISION AT GIVENCHY.
"Headquarters, France, Monday, 1-15 p.m.
"On the morning of the German attack on April 9th, 1918, the 55th (West Lancashire) Division (Terri-

torial) was holding a front of about 6,000 yards, extending from the La Bassee Canal to just South of Richebourg l'Avoue, where its line joined that held by the Portuguese. The enemy's attack on the Southern portion of this front was delivered by all three regiments of the 4th Ersatz Division, which was well up to strength. A captured Divisional Order issued by the General Staff of this German Division, and dated April 6th, 1918, shows that its objectives were 'the ground and the British position in the triangle formed by Givenchy—Festubert—Gorre.' The following passages from this captured order are of special interest :—

"'In our attack our three regiments will be opposed by at most six companies in front and at most two reserve battalions in Festubert and Givenchy. One battalion in Divisional Reserve is South of the La Bassee Canal in Le Preol. It will be prevented by our powerful artillery fire from taking part in the fight for Festubert and Givenchy. Troops are elements of the English 55th Division, which, after being engaged on the Somme, has suffered heavy losses in Flanders and at Cambrai, and was described by prisoners in March, 1918, as a Division fit to hold a quiet sector, that is below the average quality.'

"The Order containing the passages quoted above was distributed among all Officers and Under Officers of the 4th Ersatz Division down to Platoon Commanders, presumably with a view to encouraging the troops prior to their attack, and in belief that the opposition met with would not be very serious. If this was his expectation the enemy was most signally disappointed.

"Throughout the early part of the morning of April 9th the 55th Division beat off all attacks in its forward zone, and maintained its line intact. Later, when the German infantry had broken through the Portuguese positions on its left, the Division formed a defensive flank facing north-east on the line Givenchy—Festubert to the neighbourhood of Le Touret. This line it maintained practically unchanged until relief, through six days of almost continual fighting, in the course of which it beat off repeated German attacks with the heaviest losses to the enemy, and took nearly 1,000 prisoners.

"At one time, on the first day of his attack, the enemy's troops forced their way into Givenchy and Festubert. Both villages were shortly afterwards regained by the 55th Division as the result of a highly successful counter-attack, in which several hundred Germans were captured. All further attempts on the part of the enemy to carry these positions broke down before the resolute defence of the 55th Division. Though he succeeded on April 11th in entering a post north of Festubert, he was thrown out again by a counter-attack, and on the night of April 12th the 55th Division improved its position in this neighbourhood, capturing a German post and taking several prisoners.

"Next day, during the afternoon, the enemy heavily bombarded the whole front held by the Division between Gorre and the Lawe Canal, and subsequently attacked in strength. He was once more repulsed with heavy loss by the most gallant and successful defence of a Division which he had been pleased to describe as consisting of second class troops."

EXTRACT FROM THE GENERAL DESPATCH OF THE COMMANDER-IN-CHIEF.

"The possibility of a German attack north of the La Bassee Canal, for which certain preparations appeared to have been carried out, had been brought to my notice prior to March 21st. Indications that preparations for a hostile attack in this sector were nearing completion had been observed in the first days of April, but its extent and force could not be accurately gauged.

"There were obvious advantages for the enemy in such a course of action. In the first place, the depth of his advance on the southern portion of the battle front had left him with a long and dangerously exposed flank between Noyon and Montdidier. The absence of properly organised communications in the battle area made this flank peculiarly vulnerable to a counter-stroke by the French. To prevent this, and preserve the initiative in his hands, it was essential that he should renew his attack without delay.

"In the second place, the heavy and prolonged struggle on the Somme had placed a severe strain on the forces under my command, and had absorbed the whole of my reserves. Further, to meet the urgent demands of the battle, I had been forced to withdraw ten Divisions from the northern portion of my line, and to replace them by Divisions exhausted in the Somme fighting, which had only just been made up with reinforcements recently sent out from home. The Divisions thus withdrawn had been taken chiefly from the Flanders front, where, in a normal year, condition of the ground could be relied upon to make offensive operations on a large scale impossible before May at the earliest.

"A strong additional reason for drawing these Divisions principally from the north was furnished by conditions on the central portion of my front between the Scarpe and the La Bassee Canal. Should urgent necessity arise, it would be possible to give ground to a limited extent in the north, while still preserving strong lines of defence, which could in part be covered by inundations. On the other hand, a break through on our centre, about Vimy, would mean the realisation of the enemy's plan which had been foiled by our defence at Arras on March 28th—namely, the capture of Amiens and the separation of the bulk of the British Armies from the French and from those British forces acting under the direction of the latter.

"The enemy's preparations for an offensive in this central sector, the extreme importance of which will be readily understood, had been complete for some time. The admirable and extensive railway system serving it made it possible for him to effect with great rapidity at any moment the concentration of troops necessary for an attack. My own forces in this sector, therefore, could not greatly be reduced.

"In consequence of these different factors, the bulk of the Divisions in front line in the northern battle—and in particular the 40th, 34th, 25th, 19th and 9th Divisions—which on April 9th held the portion of my front between the Portuguese sector and the Ypres–Comines Canal, had already taken part in the Southern battle. It must be remembered that before the Northern battle commenced, forty-six out of my total force of fifty-eight Divisions had been engaged in the southern area.

"At the end of March, however, the northern front was rapidly drying up under the influence of the exceptionally rainless spring, and, in view of the indications referred to, the possibility of an early attack in this sector became a matter for immediate consideration. Arrangements for the relief of the Portuguese Division, which had been continuously in the line for a long period and needed rest, were therefore undertaken during the first week of April, and were to have been completed by the morning of April 10th. Meanwhile, other Divisions which had been engaged in the Somme fighting, and had been withdrawn to rest and reorganise, were moved up behind the Lys front. Arrangements had already been made for the evacuation of the salient at Passchendæle should circumstances require it, a measure which would both upset any preparations which the enemy might have made for an offensive there and economise a few troops for use elsewhere.

"The steps which I could take, however, to meet a danger which I could foresee, were limited by the fact that, though the enemy's progress on the Somme had for the time been stayed, the great mass of hostile Divisions still concentrated on that front constituted a threat to the safety of the British Armies of an imperative character. The enemy was in a position to take immediate advantage of any weakening of my forces in that area.

"THE LYS BATTLE OPENED.

"The persistence of unseasonably fine weather and the rapid drying up of the low-lying ground in the Lys Valley, enabled the enemy to anticipate the relief of the 2nd Portuguese Division.

"On the night of April 7th an unusually heavy and prolonged bombardment with gas shell was opened

PHOTOGRAPH OF PORT

OF THE GIVENCHY FRONT.

along practically the whole front from Lens to Armentieres. At about 4 a.m. on April 9th the bombardment re-commenced with the greatest intensity, with both gas and high explosive shell.

"The enemy's attack, in the first instance, was launched on the northern portion of the front of General Sir H. S. Horne's First Army, held by the XI. and XV. Corps under Command, respectively, of Lieut.-General Sir R. C. R. Haking, K.C.B., K.C.M.G., and Lieut.-General Sir J. P. Du Cane, K.C.B. On April 10th the right of General H. C. O. Plumer's Second Army, held by the IX. Corps under Command of Lieut.-General Sir A. Hamilton Gordon, K.C.B., was also involved. In the early stages of the battle the XV. Corps was transferred to the Second Army, and at later dates the extension of the battle front led to the intervention of the I. Corps, under Command of Lieut.-General Sir Arthur Holland, K.C.B., M.V.O., D.S.O., on the First Army front, and of the XXII. Corps, under the Command of Lieut.-General Sir A. J. Godley, K.C.B., K.C.M.G., on the Second Army front. Subsequently the II. Corps of the Second Army, under the Command of Lieut.-General Sir C. W. Jacob, K.C.B., became involved in the withdrawal from the Passchendæle salient.

"At about 7 a.m. on April 9th, in thick fog, which again made observation impossible, the enemy appears to have attacked the left Brigade of the 2nd Portuguese Division in strength and to have broken into their trenches. A few minutes afterwards, the area of attack spread south and north. Shortly after 7 a.m. the right Brigade of the 40th Division reported that an attack had developed on their front and was being held, but machine gunners near their right-hand post could see the enemy moving rapidly through the sector to the south of them.

"Communication with the Divisions in line was difficult, but during the morning the situation cleared up, and it became apparent that a serious attack was in progress on the front of the 55th Division, under Command of Major-General H. S. Jeudwine, C.B., and of the 2nd Portuguese and 40th Divisions, from the La Bassee Canal to Bois Grenier. Meanwhile, shortly after the opening of the bombardment, orders had been given to the 51st and 50th Divisions to move up behind Richebourg St. Vaast and Laventie, and take up their positions in accordance with the pre-arranged Defence Scheme. Both these Divisions had also been heavily engaged in the Somme battle, and had but recently arrived in the neighbourhood. The 1st King Edward's Horse and the 11th Cyclist Battalion had been sent forward at once to cover their deployment.

"Between 8 a.m. and 9 a.m. the enemy succeeded in occupying the forward posts of the right battalion of the 40th Division, and attacked northwards along the Rue Petillon and the Rue de Bois. Our machine gun posts in this area continued to fight until all but one of their machine guns were destroyed, and by their fire greatly delayed this progress. At 10-15 a.m., however, his troops were already in Rouge de Bout, more than 2,000 yards in rear of the Headquarters of the 40th Division's right battalion, which, at this hour, were still holding out at Petillon. Later in the morning the 40th Division was pushed back by pressure on its front and flank, to a position facing south between Bois Grenier, Fleurbaix, and Sailly-Sur-La-Lys, its right Brigade, in particular, having lost heavily.

"South of the Portuguese sector, the 55th Division was heavily attacked on its whole front, and by 10-30 a.m. its left Brigade had been forced back from its outpost line. The main line of resistance was intact, and a defensive flank was formed facing north between Festubert and the strong point just south of Le Touret, where touch was established later with troops of the 51st Division.

"Throughout the remainder of the day, the 55th Division maintained its positions against all assaults, and by successful counter-attacks captured over 750 prisoners. The success of this most gallant defence, the importance of which it would be hard to over-estimate, was due in great measure to the courage and determination displayed by our advanced posts. These held out with the utmost resolution, though surrounded, pinning to the ground those parties of the enemy who had penetrated our defences, and preventing them from developing their attacks. Among the many gallant deeds recorded of them, one instance is known of a machine gun which was kept in action although the German infantry had entered the rear compartment of the 'Pill Box' from which it was firing, the gun team holding up the enemy by revolver fire from the inner compartment.

"To the north of the positions held by the 55th Division, the weight and impetus of the German attack overwhelmed the Portuguese troops, and the enemy's progress was so rapid that the arrangements for manning the rear defences of this sector with British troops could scarcely be completed in time."

The Division was not destined to remain for long in the rest area, for, on the 21st April, the 166th

Infantry Brigade, together with one Company of the 55th Battalion Machine Gun Corps, were moved up by lorry into the forward area and came temporarily under the command of the 1st Division. On this same day the Division received a visit from M. Clemenceau, the French Minister of War, and on this day also the 2/10th Liverpool Scottish arrived from the 57th Division for amalgamation with the 1/10th Liverpool Scottish. The day following, this battalion proceeded to Gorre to join the 166th Infantry Brigade. On the 22nd and 23rd of April the Division returned to the line and relieved the 1st Division in the Givenchy and Festubert sections.

While the Division had been out resting, the enemy had made yet another attempt to gain possession of Route A Keep, and this time had succeeded in capturing it. Our first duty, therefore, on returning to the line, was to turn him out again, and the task was confided to the Liverpool Scottish, who, on the 24th, not only re-captured the Keep, but took ten of the garrison prisoners, together with one heavy and three light machine guns. Having re-captured the Keep, its further custody passed from our hands to the 46th Division, who that day became responsible for this portion of the line. But although we had ceased to be responsible for the Keep, we none the less took great interest in its tenure, and we anticipated that the enemy would not leave it permanently in the possession of our troops without further attempts to regain it. We were not, therefore, surprised to hear that on April 26th, after a very heavy barrage on the Keep, the enemy had once again attacked and once again had retaken it. Two days later he was again turned out, and henceforward the Keep remained in British hands. It had been attacked and counter-attacked no fewer than eight times. On 18th April another strong attack had been launched against Givenchy, but had been bloodily repulsed by the 1st Division. The enemy, however, succeeded in occupying our original front line in that neighbourhood and the Givenchy Craters, and remained in possession of them till we attacked and regained them on the 24th August.

In this attack on April 18th the Field Artillery and Trench Mortar Batteries of the Division—which had remained in the line to assist the 1st Division—played a very important part, and subsequently received the following compliment from the Corps Commander:—

" From Lieut.-General Sir A. Holland, K.C.B.,
" M.V.O., D.S.O.,
" Commanding I. Corps.
" 21/4/18.

" The Corps Commander wishes to place on record his high appreciation of the work done by the Trench Artillery of the 55th Division during the attack on Givenchy on the 18th April. The detachments, by their heroic stand, assisted materially in the retention of the Givenchy position, and have added another page to the glorious history of the Royal Regiment of Artillery."

Shortly after dark on the 25th of April, two raiding parties went out to endeavour to occupy the junctions of Orchard and Finchley Roads with our old front line, but found the enemy alert and established in force. Our parties, in consequence, became heavily engaged and were driven back. At 11-15 p.m., under cover of an artillery barrage, a detachment of the 1/4th King's Own

Royal Lancasters again attacked the position, but could make no progress owing to the heavy machine gun fire. A further attack by two platoons, and with an increased barrage, was made at 4 a.m., and this detachment succeeded in reaching the enemy's positions, where heavy fighting took place. Our troops were, however, subsequently compelled to withdraw, but they had inflicted severe casualties on the enemy, especially by rifle and machine gun fire from Death and Glory Sap, where arrangements had been made to deal with any reinforcements the enemy might bring across No Man's Land.

The following afternoon a more important operation took place. As has already been stated, the enemy, during the period when the Division had been out resting, had succeeded in capturing from the Division which had relieved us the very important posts in the Craters in our old front line. These Crater posts gave the enemy observation over our front, and at the same time deprived us of observation of his front. It was urgent that, if possible, these crater posts should be re-captured, and at 2-20 p.m. on the 26th, under cover of a heavy barrage, two companies—one from the 1/4th King's Own Royal Lancasters and one from the 2/5th Lancashire Fusiliers—were committed to the attempt. The right company, the 1/4th King's Own, succeeded in gaining its objective, but the Fusiliers, owing to the fact that the barrage did not come down on K and J Saps, failed to take these Saps, and though they had made progress on their right flank, our men were forced to fight their way back. The fighting was of the fiercest description, and, in addition to causing the enemy severe casualties in killed and wounded, our men brought back 37 prisoners.

On the 2nd May a great increase was noted in the activity of the enemy aircraft, and other indications that an attack upon our front was in contemplation, and, indeed, was imminent, were noticed. Prisoners whom we had captured, and deserters who had come over to our lines, asserted that a strong enemy attack would take place soon after the 9th May, and other information which came to hand seemed to confirm this. Our artillery therefore increased its harassment of roads, dumps, back areas, and possible concentration points, and on the 8th of May a shoot with aeroplane observation was carried out upon the great ammunition dump at Salome. This shoot was completely successful, and at 5 p.m. the dump was blown up. Prisoners subsequently captured stated that the explosion of the Salome dump had caused 50 casualties to the enemy. The following day a similar shoot, with aeroplane observation, was carried out upon Lacouture Church, which was being used by the enemy as an observation post. Again the shoot was a success and the church was destroyed.

Meantime all precautions were taken and dispositions made to meet the enemy attack which obviously was coming and could not long be delayed. The reserve troops were ordered to stand-to each night until after dawn, and double harassing fire on the enemy approaches, assembly areas, and centres of activity, was carried out each night. This procedure was continued until the 15th of May, when it became plain that something had gone seriously wrong with the enemy's plans, and that the attack, for the time being at all events, was postponed. Whether this postponement was due to the intensity of our harassing fire, which is known to have caused the enemy heavy casualties when endeavouring to assemble his troops for the attack, or whether, as subsequently stated by him, the postponement was due to the prevalence of a very severe epidemic of influenza among his troops, cannot be stated here. That a serious attack was contemplated is, however, quite certain. We were quite ready for it, and quite confident of the result.

During the remainder of the month of May events proceeded normally. On June 4th, however, both Beuvry and Givenchy sections were heavily bombarded with gas shells, and during the following night both Beuvry and Labourse were heavily shelled with Yellow Cross. Prisoners having stated that a hostile attack upon the Divisional front was imminent, precautionary measures were taken and the necessary dispositions made. No attack, however, took place, and on June 8th at 12-30 a.m. a raiding party of the 2/5th Lancashire Fusiliers attempted to rush the enemy shell hole positions on their front and to secure identifications. The enemy, however, was found to be very much on the alert, and our parties were in consequence unable to affect an entry into the enemy trenches.

Things subsequently remained normal, with occasional small raids, until August 24th, when events on other fronts seemed to indicate that the moment had now come for an attack upon the long-coveted Craters, and an advance through the enemy's defence system. The method and progress of that advance will be described in the chapter which follows.

On the 19th of September the I. Corps was transferred from the First to the Fifth Army, and the following letter from the Army Commander was received by the Division :—

" To-day the I. Corps leaves the First Army, and severs a connection which has existed since the formation of the latter in December, 1914.

" I wish to thank you, your Staff, Division and other Commanders, and all ranks, for the loyal support that has been given to me in every way, tactical and administrative, great or small, throughout the two years during which I have had the honour to command the First Army.

" In 1917 the troops of the I. Corps, although holding an extended front, materially assisted the operations of the Canadian Corps, which resulted in the capture of the Vimy Ridge. The 24th Division seized the Bois en Hache, clearing the eastern end of the Notre Dame De Lorette, and, after much street fighting in Angres and Lieven, gained the important positions about the Bois Riaumont. The 46th Division captured Reservoir Hill, and the 6th Division advanced their line considerably towards Hill 70. All this was accomplished by local troops without reinforcements.

" In 1918, the I. Corps front, a salient position covering the area of the coal mines, assumed vital importance during the spring and early summer. A successful attack on this front would have given the Germans advantages which might have affected very seriously the course of events. The splendid defence of Givenchy by the 55th Division on April 9th, and again by the 1st Division on April 18th, were events of first class importance, which—combined with the thoroughness of the defensive work carried out with such energy along the frontage of the Corps by the 11th and 46th Divisions— impressed upon the German Command the inadvisability of launching the attacks for which preparations had, without doubt, been made by them.

"Following up with energy the weakening of the enemy consequent upon his defeats elsewhere, the 55th, 16th and 15th Divisions have succeeded in ousting the Germans from such strong positions as Givenchy Craters, the Railway Triangle, Auchy, Fosse 8, and the Quarries.

"The I. Corps has nobly maintained the reputation gained in the opening days of the war.

"I hand over the I. Corps with great regret—but what is the First Army's loss is the Fifth Army's gain—and I am confident that, whatever the conditions under which the I. Corps may find itself, the same spirit will remain, and it will act up to its traditions.

"H. S. HORNE,
"General,
"First Army, "Commanding First Army.
"19th September, 1918."

On October 8th the Division was transferred to the III. Corps, and on leaving, the following letter was received from the G. O. C., I. Corps :—

"On the transfer of the 55th Division to the III. Corps, I wish to express my thanks to Major-General Sir Hugh Jeudwine and all ranks of the Division, for the good work done during the 11 months which they have been in the I. Corps. During the last year on every occasion on which they have been called upon the 55th Division have shown the highest fighting spirit, which, combined with the high standard of tactical training and discipline displayed by all ranks, has invariably led to success. I would especially mention the defence of Givenchy in April, 1918, when the heroic stand made by the Division prevented the Bethune coal fields from being over-run by the enemy; and the persistent and energetic following up of the enemy when he withdrew, in September and October, from the Givenchy front to the Haute Deule Canal. This energetic pursuit considerably hastened the enemy's retirement, caused him loss, and saved many villages from complete destruction. In bidding goodbye to the Division I wish all ranks every success, and feel confident that they will on all occasions not only maintain but add to the high traditions of the 55th Division.

"A. E. A. HOLLAND,
"Lieut.-General,
"Commanding I. Corps.

"8th October, 1918."

CHAPTER VI.

THE CAPTURE OF THE CRATERS AND THE ADVANCE.

On the morning of August 24th, 1918, the Division held the Givenchy—Festubert section, and was distributed as follows :—

Right Brigade Section. 164*th Infantry Brigade.*
Right Battalion.   1/4th K.O. Royal Lancaster Regt.
Left Battalion.   2/5th Lancashire Fusiliers.
Support Battalion. 1/4th Loyal North Lancs. Regt.

Left Brigade Section. 166*th Infantry Brigade.*
Right Battalion.   1/5th K.O. Royal Lancaster Regt.
Left Battalion.   1/5th South Lancashire Regt.
Support Battalion. Liverpool Scottish.

Reserve Brigade. 165*th Infantry Brigade.*
1/5th King's Liverpool Regt.
1/6th King's Liverpool Regt.
1/7th King's Liverpool Regt.

The Right Brigade Section was supported by the 276th Brigade R.F.A. and by "C" Company, 55th Battalion M.G.C. The Left Brigade was supported by the 275th Brigade R.F.A. and by "D" Company, 55th Battalion M.G.C.

For some time past a scheme had been under consideration for re-taking the line of Craters east of Givenchy. These Craters occupied a position which commanded an excellent view of ground to the east, and their occupation by the enemy not only denied to us this advantage, but also gave to him observation over a large portion of our defensive system.

The 24th August was fixed for the operation, which was entrusted to the Brigadier-General Commanding the 164th Infantry Brigade, who had at his disposal the 164th Infantry Brigade, the Divisional Artillery, the 84th and 158th Army Brigades R.F.A., two batteries of Artillery from the 1st Division, Heavy Artillery, the 55th Battalion Machine Gun Corps, a proportion of the Divisional Engineers and Pioneers, and a portion of the 3rd Australian Tunnelling Company.

The hour fixed for the attack was 7-20 a.m. The attack was carried out by the 1/4th King's Own Royal Lancaster Regiment on the right, with objective from Warlingham Crater to the most northern of the " E " Sap Craters; the 2/5th Lancashire Fusiliers on the left, with objective the Craters from " E " Sap Craters to " K " Sap Crater, with subsidiary attacks on New Rose Trench and the old British line. The 1/4th Loyal North Lancs. were to hold strong points behind our original front line. The 166th Infantry Brigade were to co-operate by sending a party to establish a post up Cheshire Road. The morning was rainy. No bombardment of any kind was put down by us until five minutes after zero hour.

The enemy was taken completely by surprise, and his resistance was feeble. By 8 a.m. all objectives had been taken, and an outpost line pushed forward about 200 yards east of the Craters. The number of prisoners taken was 38 unwounded and six wounded, and the estimated number of enemy killed was four Officers and 30 other ranks. Our casualties were 20 killed and three Officers and 80 other ranks wounded.

Only two weak counter-attacks were made, both of which were driven off without difficulty, and although

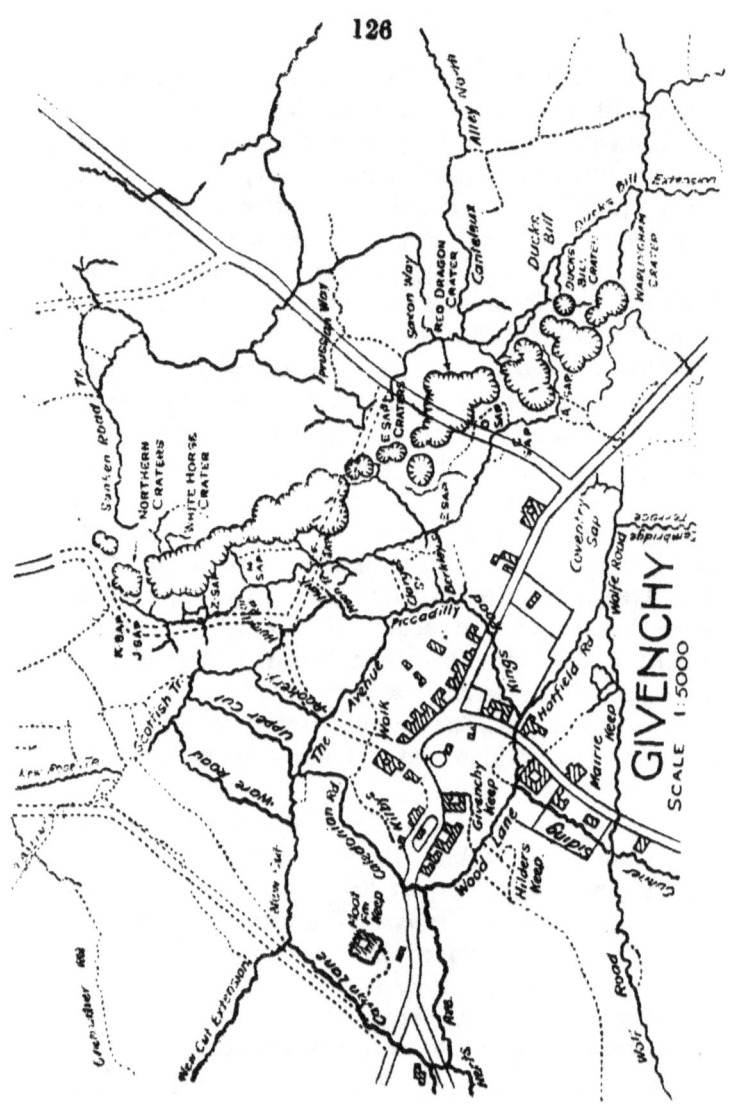

the crater area was for some days subjected to fairly heavy bombardment with H.E. and gas, no serious attempt was ever made by the enemy to re-take the ground he had lost. The result of the operation was to place us in possession of ground which had never previously been in British hands. It also necessitated the adjustment of the line of resistance so as to include the eastern lips of the craters. As this entailed making our front line, in places, our line of resistance, Brigades were ordered to endeavour to push forward their outposts, so as to form a line of posts well to the east of the Craters.

On August 28th the 166th Infantry Brigade found Festubert East Keep unoccupied by the enemy, and took possession of it.

During the last days of August, events on other fronts led to the belief that the enemy might be compelled to retire on the Divisional front. Reports of fires and explosions behind his line strengthened this belief, and on the morning of August 30th the 46th Division on our left reported that, as a result of an enemy withdrawal from the north, they had advanced their line and had occupied Lacouture. Prisoners stated that a retirement to a line running through Richebourg—St. Vaast was about to take place.

In accordance with instructions received from the I. Corps, orders were issued, on September 1st, for Infantry Brigades in the line to be prepared to follow up the enemy rapidly, should the withdrawal which had taken place to the north extend to the Divisional front. There was to be no attempt to maintain a continuous line during such an advance, but fighting patrols were to make good what ground they could on pre-determined plans co-ordinated by Brigadiers. The Divisional Artillery was ordered to be prepared to push forward guns to successive positions to cover any advance. Pack trains were to be organised for supply of rations and ammunition. Two roads were to be made good for horsed transport, namely, Estaminet Corner—Ration Corner—Festubert—Quinque Rue, and Westminster Bridge—Lone Farm—Windy Corner—Givenchy.

Consequent on these orders numerous patrols worked forward, both by day and night, during September 2nd, from the Infantry Brigades in the line (165th Infantry Brigade Givenchy Section; 166th Infantry Brigade Festubert Section). These patrols succeeded in establishing posts about 500 yards east of the Craters and Festubert, with only slight opposition, although it was apparent that no considerable retirement of the enemy was yet in progress on the Divisional front.

Patrols continued to advance during September 3rd, and 165th Infantry Brigade (which had relieved 166th Infantry Brigade in the left section on the night 2nd/3rd September) had by 10 p.m. occupied the whole of the old British line as far north as Shetland Road, and were established in Indian Village, also at Barnton Tee, Princes' Island and Old Man's Corner in the old German trenches, taking 19 prisoners. During September 4th, 5th and 6th, patrols were continually pressing forward, meeting with gradually increasing resistance, and by the morning of September 7th our line consisted of posts established on the general line Canal Reserve—northern part of Canteleux Trench—Violaines Trench—Dover Reserve—Marsden Keep, with forward posts down Towpath Alley—Plain Alley—Canteleux Alley N. and S.—La Bassee Alley—southern outskirts of Violaines.

Photo by Bowley, Tunbridge Wells

Lt.-Col. B. FAIRCLOUGH, C.M.G., D.S.O., T D.
1/4th South Lancashire Regt.

Photo by Kay, Bolton

Lt.-Col. C. E. WALKER, D.S.O.
275th Brigade, R.F.A.

Photo by Beresford, London, S.W.

Major W. N. PILKINGTON, D.S.O.
1/5th South Lancashire Regt.

Photo by Bacon & Sons, Liverpool

Lt.-Col. J. R. DAVIDSON, C.M.G.
Liverpool Scottish.

On the left the 46th Division had continued to press forward with patrols, and, when relieved by the 19th Division on September 6th, our line was in touch with them at Cour D'Avoue Farm. On the right the 16th Division met with considerable opposition, and, although they succeeded in advancing their line in their southern section on September 5th, the resistance met with just south of the La Bassee Canal was such as to prevent their advance in that area. This had a considerable effect on the action of our right Brigade, for, so long as the enemy held Railway Triangle and Embankment Redoubt, any posts which we could establish in the southern portion of Canteleux Trench were enfiladed from the high embankment to the south.

In addition to this difficulty our advance at this period was rendered slower by reason of the fact that the hostile resistance had stiffened considerably, and it was uncertain whether the enemy intended to hold the La Bassee—Fromelles line in strength, which would have necessitated a deliberate attack, which our higher command was not at this time prepared to undertake, or whether a retirement was intended to the Haute Deule Canal, a movement which prisoners had stated was in contemplation.

On September 7th the 164th Infantry Brigade made an attempt to capture the southern part of Canteleux Trench and Apse House. The attack was only partially successful, and a strong enemy counter-attack, estimated at 200 men, drove back our posts to their original positions. During the period September 7th—September 12th patrols from the 165th Brigade continued to push forward, meeting considerable numbers of the enemy, and being engaged in severe hand-to-hand fighting. By September 12th posts had been established in La Bassee Alley—Marais Alley—Eitel Alley South—Adalbert Alley—Junction of Serpent and Solace Trenches. In each case the enemy held posts at blocks in these trenches in close contact with our posts. During the same period our posts in the right Brigade section in Canteleux Alley South, Plain Alley and Towpath Alley had been several times attacked by the enemy, who still held Canteleux Trench and Apse House. All attempts to push forward to Canteleux Trench were met with strong resistance, and any bombardment of enemy posts in this area brought down heavy retaliation.

On September 11th the 16th Division on our right carried out an operation which left them in possession of the Railway Triangle. This rendered our positions in Canal Reserve and posts in the communication trenches east of this more easily tenable ; but so long as the enemy held the high railway embankment east of Railway Triangle, the taking and holding of Canteleux Trench was still a difficult operation.

On September 14th 164th Infantry Brigade (two companies 2/5th Lancashire Fusiliers) in the right section made another attempt to capture Canteleux Trench, in conjunction with 16th Division, who were to push forward and establish posts on the embankment south of the Canal at a point about opposite to the southern extremity of Canteleux Trench. The operation was at first partially successful, but a heavy artillery retaliation, followed by a strong counter-attack, drove our posts back to their original line. In this operation the 2/5th Lancashire Fusiliers fought continuously for six hours before being forced back. The 16th Division were also forced back to their original line.

On the same day a minor operation by 166th Infantry Brigade in the left section succeeded in advancing our posts about 400 yards.

With the exception of the slight advance of posts in the left section, there was no material change in the situation until September 17th, on which date an operation was undertaken by the 165th Infantry Brigade (which had relieved the 164th Infantry Brigade in the right section), again with the object of capturing Canteleux Trench. The attack was carried out by four companies of the 1/5th King's Liverpool Regiment. The 16th Division on the right co-operated with the object of establishing posts on the south of the Canal, in touch and level with our final objective. A preliminary bombardment of the objective was carried out by Corps Heavy Artillery. All the Divisional Artillery was placed at the disposal of B.G.C. 165th Infantry Brigade for the operation, which commenced at 5-30 a.m. The attack was completely successful, with very slight casualties. The whole of the southern portion of Canteleux Trench and Apse House were captured, and advanced posts were pushed forward in Towpath Alley and Apse Road. The 16th Division gained all their objectives on our right, and established posts in touch with us just south of the Canal and level with the southern end of Canteleux Trench. In the afternoon of the same day an enemy counter-attack south of the Canal drove the 16th Division back from the posts they had established, and for a time Canteleux Trench was enfiladed by enemy machine guns from their old positions on the embankment. The situation was, however, restored later in the day, when the 16th Division re-took the posts they had lost. On the 18th

September an enemy counter-attack of about 60 men developed against our new positions and our post at the junction of Apse Road and Canteleux Alley South was temporarily lost, but was re-established.

This ended the fighting for Canteleux Trench, the capture of which gave us observation over the ground between that trench and the La Bassee—Fromelles line. Information as to the intention of the enemy to hold the latter line was still obscure. Prisoners had stated that a withdrawal to the Haute Deule Canal was contemplated. On the other hand the resistance offered to all attempts to push posts forward towards the La Bassee—Fromelles line was stiffening.

On September 19th the I. Corps, including the Division, was transferred from the First to the Fifth Army.

On September 20th the left Brigade (166th Infantry Brigade) carried out a minor operation in conjunction with the 19th Division on our left. The objective of the 19th Division was the La Bassee Road from its junction with Mitzi Trench to the Distillery (both inclusive). The objective of the 166th Infantry Brigade was the Pumping Stations to the junction of Serpent and Nora Trenches. The attack was carried out by two companies of the 1/5th South Lancashire Regiment, and was timed to commence at 6-30 a.m. The attack was successful, both on our front and on that of the 19th Division, and all objectives were gained, 43 unwounded prisoners being captured by the 1/5th South Lancashire Regiment. On the same morning the 165th Infantry Brigade in the right section occupied Belt, Button and Braces Trenches, and pushed patrols into Violaines, La Bassee Alley South and Roch Alley, close up to the La Bassee—Aubers line.

On the night of September 20th/21st the 164th Infantry Brigade relieved the 165th Infantry Brigade in the right section, and, in accordance with I. Corps orders, took over one Battalion front from the 16th Division south of the La Bassee Canal.

The enemy counter-attacked the right of the 19th Division on September 22nd, and re-took the Distillery and Nora Trench; our post at the junction of Nora and Serpent Trenches also withdrew to the Drain in front of Spook Trench. The 19th Division arranged to attack again, with the object of regaining the ground lost, but the attack was postponed until September 25th.

The policy which had formed the basis of the action on the Divisional front since the taking of the Givenchy Craters on August 24th had now for the time being served its purpose—that is to say a deep outpost zone had been established east of the main line of resistance. The eastern edge of the outpost line consisted of mutually supporting posts along the general line, eastern limit of Railway Triangle—Canteleux Trench—Violaines—Strong Farm—Flat Farm—Pumping Stations—Spook Trench. The main line of resistance was now advanced on the left so as to run along the eastern edge of the Givenchy Craters, and thence northward along the old British front line. The hostile resistance having necessarily increased as the La Bassee—Fromelles line was approached, orders were issued that indiscriminate establishing of advanced posts was to be avoided, and that the outpost line was to be strengthened. This precaution was considered necessary owing to the possibility of a hostile counter-attack in strength being launched from behind the La Bassee—Fromelles line, which was a strong line and, as far as could be ascertained, fairly strongly held. At the same time infantry brigades in the line were ordered to be active in patrolling in front of the outpost zone, in order to detect immediately any signs of enemy withdrawal, and, in order that troops might be readily available for following up quickly, B.Gs.C. were informed that they might dispose two whole battalions in the outpost zone.

The Divisional Artillery was disposed so as to cover the main line of resistance, and at the same time support any further advance.

On September 23rd Divisional Headquarters moved forward from Drouvin to Gosnay.

The 19th Division carried out an operation on September 25th, to regain the line of the La Bassee—Estaires Road, including the Distillery and Shepherd's Redoubt. 165th Infantry Brigade, which had relieved 166th Infantry Brigade in the left section on the night of September 23rd/24th, was to co-operate in this attack, and the objectives of the Brigade were more extended than in the previous operation of September 19th, so as to include the La Bassee—Estaires Road as far south as Telephone Exchange. The operation began at 8 a.m. and was carried out by one battalion (1/6th King's Liverpool Regiment). All objectives were taken, and at 10-30 a.m. a weak counter-attack was driven off. At 6-30 p.m., however, the enemy, after a heavy bombardment, again counter-attacked, and re-took the line of the La Bassee Road from the Telephone Exchange northward to the Divisional boundary. At 3-30 a.m. on September 26th the 1/6th King's Liverpool Regiment attacked again, and re-established our posts along the La Bassee—Estaires Road as before. As a result of the fighting on these two days our left Brigade and the right Brigade of the 19th Division had posts established on the east side of the La Bassee—Estaires Road from the Telephone Exchange northward, and 105 prisoners were taken by the 1/6th King's Liverpool Regiment at a cost of only 52 casualties.

From the Telephone Exchange southward the right of the 165th Infantry Brigade was thrown back through the Pumping Stations. A minor operation was therefore planned for the early morning of September 27th, with the object of bringing up the right flank to the La Bassee —Estaires Road from Telephone Exchange to Piano House. The attack was carried out at 2-55 a.m. by three companies of the 1/5th King's Liverpool Regiment, and was completely successful. The line gained however was subjected to very heavy hostile artillery fire on the following day, and on September 29th, after a heavy bombardment, an attack was launched by a Sturm Battalion, and our posts were forced back from Piano House and Saucy Trench. Later in the morning of the same day our posts were re-established, with the exception of that at Piano House, and at 3 p.m. the 1/7th King's Liverpool Regiment re-captured the whole of Saucy Trench and Piano House.

The I. Corps issued instructions on September 27th to the effect that the enemy was believed to have made all arrangements for a withdrawal on the Fifth Army front. All Divisions in the Corps were to push forward posts simultaneously south of the La Bassee Canal on the morning of September 30th, after 24 hours of harassing artillery fire, commencing on September 28th. In accordance with these instructions, two companies of the 1/4th Loyal North Lancashire Regiment attacked south of the Canal at 6-18 a.m. on September

30th. The objectives of the attack were Canal Alley—Junction of Drain and Azimuth Alley—Distillery ; the last named was a strong place and believed to be used as an enemy O.P. The attack was at first successful, and all objectives gained, with 48 prisoners. The 16th Division on our right were unable to make headway against strong opposition, and at 12 noon a strong enemy counter-attack drove back the posts of the 1/4th Loyal North Lancashire Regiment to their original line after very severe fighting, in which our casualties were heavy.

On the morning of October 1st the 1/4th Loyal North Lancashire Regiment repeated the attack, and gained and held all the objectives, the 16th Division pushing forward posts on our right in touch with us.

By the end of September our line had been advanced about 4,000 yards in the Left Brigade section and about 2,500 yards in the Right Brigade section. The outpost line was 1,000 yards west of La Bassee. Three hundred and eight prisoners and 17 machine guns were captured during the month.

Events on other Army fronts at this period were developing greatly in our favour, and a general policy was laid down to the effect that Divisions in the I. Corps were to be organised so as to be able to follow up rapidly should any considerable enemy retirement take place. At the same time it was intimated that the number of Divisions available in the Fifth Army did not warrant the assumption of offensive operations on a large scale against the enemy in strong defensive positions. The I. Corps laid down the following general lines to be reached successively in the event of the enemy withdrawing :—

(1) Bois de Dix Huit—Hulluch—Cite St. Elie—Haisnes—La Bassee—Illies.

(2) Bois de Quatorze—Benifontaine—Douvrin—Salome—Petit Moisnil—Marquillies.

In order to enable Brigades in the line to put the above policy into effect when opportunity arose, they were organised each as one advanced guard and a main body, and the following troops of all arms were placed at the disposal of each of the Brigadiers Commanding Infantry Brigades in the line :—

(a) One Section of " C " Squadron King Edward's Horse.

(b) One Section R.E.

(c) One 18-pdr. Battery ; one Section 4.5" Howitzers, and one Section Medium Trench Mortars (the last named had been made mobile on extemporised carriages constructed from G.S. limbered wagons).

(d) One Company Machine Gun Battalion.

(e) A proportion of a Field Ambulance.

(f) An Investigation Party. (These were personnel of Tunnelling Companies, and were rendered necessary owing to the large number of enemy traps left in dug-outs and in roads. They rendered throughout most valuable assistance, and saved a large number of casualties).

The Divisional policy laid down was that on the code word " Scurry " being sent out from Divisional Headquarters, the troops of all arms shown above should proceed to positions of assembly previously arranged by B.Gs.C., while the Reserve Brigade moved to positions of readiness, which were notified. The " Scurry " telegram was also to contain the Divisional objective for the main bodies of Brigades in the line, and the hour at which the advance was to begin. The advanced guards of Brigades were to push beyond the objective, and, as soon as this had been done, the main line of resistance and its garrison were to be moved to the objective reached by the main body of the Brigades in the line. The advance was thus to be in depth, and if a check occurred the advanced guard would automatically become the outpost battalion.

As events turned out, the method of withdrawal of the enemy did not enable the Corps to issue any definite order for an advance at a particular time, and, consequently, the "Scurry" telegram was never issued from Divisional H.Q. The organisation of Brigades in the line into advanced guards of all arms and a main body, however, proved very suitable to the circumstances, and the subsequent advance was on very much the same lines as it had been previously; that is to say, it was carried out by continuous pressure on enemy rearguards and by seizing opportunities for pushing forward without bringing on a general engagement of the Division.

In preparation for the continuation of the advance the following roads were made fit for horse transport by the R.E. and Pioneers, and the work done on these roads was so efficient that no delay was caused through lack of transport facilities:—

(1) La Bassee Road south of the Canal.
(2) Westminster Bridge—Windy Corner, from whence a new road was built to Chapelle St. Roch—Canteleux—Apse Road—La Bassee.
(3) Quinque Rue—Rue Du Marais.

In addition the road Barnton Tee—Redoubt Alley (South)—Rue Du Marais was made good for a pack animal track.

On October 2nd information was received from a captured German Officer that the expected withdrawal to the Haute Deule Canal had begun at 4 a.m. that morning.

Advanced Guard Battalions of 164th Infantry Brigade in the right section and 166th Infantry Brigade in the left section at once went forward, and at 1 p.m. the La Bassee—Fromelles line had been occupied without serious opposition, except in front of La Bassee, which the 2/5th Lancashire Fusiliers did not enter until the afternoon of October 2nd. By 8 p.m. the same evening our Advanced Guard Battalions were in possession of the La Bassee—Fournes Road, and were east of La Bassee with patrols in Salome, which was reported to be unoccupied.

During October 3rd and 4th the Advanced Guard Battalion continued to make ground rapidly without serious opposition. By the evening of October 3rd the following villages were occupied: Berclau, Hantay, Petit Hantay, Grand Moisnil, Marquillies, Hocron, with patrols in Sainghim-en-Weppes, where they were in touch with the Division on our left. The only opposition met with was by the 166th Infantry Brigade on the Hocron Road and in front of Grand Moisnil, and by the 164th Infantry Brigade at Petit Hantay. In the former case the opposition was overcome by pushing forward and occupying Hocron and by the expert handling of the Advanced Guard Battery with the 166th Infantry Brigade; and in the latter case an artillery bombardment by the Advanced Guard Battery of the 164th Infantry Brigade enabled the 2/5th Lancashire Fusiliers to enter Petit Hantay. By the evening of October 4th our line ran from just north of Berclau, parallel with, and about 500 yards west of, the Haute Deule Canal, as far as opposite to Don, and from there along the west side of the La Bassee—Lille railway line to the Divisional boundary. Any advance of patrols east of this line was met with heavy machine gun fire from both banks of the Haute Deule Canal, and it became evident that the enemy was in a strong position, and that his withdrawal had for the time being ceased.

During October 3rd and 4th there had been an advance of about 5 miles. All the villages occupied were in good condition, and many of them contained a considerable amount of enemy war material. There was very little fighting during these days; the enemy was never found in position in trenches, nor was his artillery fire very active at this period. In the country occupied all dug-outs had been either blown up or prepared with delay action fuses or with " booby traps "; the roads east of Salome were mined in some cases, but on the whole were in good condition and undamaged. On the other hand, the roads which had to be traversed west of Salome were badly damaged by the enemy and were very heavily cratered. In spite of this, little delay was occasioned, owing to the efficient and rapid work of the Field Companies and Pioneers, who filled as many as 32 large craters and made good 14 miles of road. In many cases mines which it had evidently been intended to blow before retiring had been left unblown. It as probable that the quickness with which our advanced guards were able to follow the enemy saved a good deal of destruction, both of private property and of war material.

The enemy's position was on the east side of the Haute Deule Canal, with a few posts on the west bank. He had a very large number of machine guns on the Canal, and was particularly active from the following places:—Canal Tee Bridge, the Laundry, Don Railway Station. Permanent bridges over the Canal had been destroyed, but many temporary foot-bridges existed. The difficulty of forcing the Canal was further increased by the fact that the enemy began to flood the low ground on the west bank, more particularly in the southern section of the Divisional front.

The policy of not undertaking an attack on a large scale against the enemy in position was necessarily still in force; consequently a period of stationary warfare now ensued for a week, until October 13th. During this week artillery and machine gun harassing fire was employed by us daily on a considerable scale, but no serious infantry action took place, with the exception of an attack by a Company of the Liverpool Scottish, 166th Infantry Brigade, on some Pill Boxes and the Railway Embankment close to Don Station. The attack was at first successful; the Pill Boxes were captured, the enemy retiring from them, and the Embankment was reached. Later, however, the enemy assembled behind a high embankment and re-took the ground won, completely cutting off and capturing most of the two platoons on the Embankment, and inflicting serious casualties.

On October 6th the main line of resistance was advanced to the general line east of Salome—east of Petit Moisnil—west of Grand Moisnil—east of Marquillies.

On October 8th the Division was transferred, in its existing position, from I. Corps to III. Corps.

By the 10th October the situation was still unchanged; patrols everywhere found the enemy in position along the Canal, and the floods continued to rise. The hostile artillery fire had considerably increased, and many fires and explosions were taking place daily behind the enemy lines. The III. Corps decided that it might be necessary to force the passage of the Haute Deule Canal by an operation on all the Corps front. A plan was, therefore, prepared for the forcing of the Canal at Don by the 165th Infantry Brigade. The 74th Division, which had replaced the 19th Division on our left, on October 3rd, was to be prepared to force the passage simultaneously at Haubourdin. On the night of October 10th/11th the Divisional front was extended northward so as to include Wavrin and Lattre.

On October 13th information was obtained from prisoners that a general retirement behind Lille was to take place that night. Patrols were at once sent out all along the Divisional front, but in every case the enemy was found to be holding his normal posts.

With a view to obtaining information prior to any attempt to force the passage of the Canal at Don, four platoons of the 1/5th King's Liverpool Regiment (165th Infantry Brigade—Right Section) carried out a raid at 9-30 p.m. on October 14th against enemy posts on the Railway Sidings south and south-west of Don Station. The raid was successful and 20 prisoners were captured. These prisoners stated that a withdrawal was expected daily, but had no knowledge of any date having been fixed.

Later in the day of October 14th, troops of the Corps on our right succeeded in crossing the Canal at Pont-a-Vendin and Meurchin; on our left the 74th Division had also advanced as a result of an enemy withdrawal. On the Divisional front, however, patrols found the enemy still in his old posts on the west bank of the Canal, and an attempt of a patrol of the 1/4th Loyal North Lancashire Regiment to capture Les Sarteaux during the night 14th/15th October failed. On the following morning, in view of the enemy withdrawal on the fronts of the Divisions on our flanks, Advanced Guard Battalions again pressed forward with patrols, but everywhere they were met with heavy machine gun fire from the old hostile posts west of the Canal. In the afternoon of the same day, however, as a result of very vigorous action on the part of patrols from the two Advanced Guard Battalions (1/5th King's Liverpool Regiment in Right Section, 1/4th Loyal North Lancashire Regiment in Left Section), the enemy was driven from all his posts west of the Canal south of Don, from Don Station and Sidings, and from Les Sarteaux. By the evening of 15th October our patrols were in touch all along the Divisional front with the enemy, who was holding the eastern bank of the Canal, with some posts still west of the Canal north-east of Don. On our right, the I. Corps had reached a line 3,000 yards east of the Haute Deule Canal, and the line of the 74th Division on our left ran through Maugres and Santes.

Arrangements had been made by the C.R.E. for bridging the Canal and dykes as follows :—Each Infantry Brigade in the line had three light foot-bridges, each capable of division into three bridges of 21 feet span, and each loaded on three G.S. wagons ; in addition, each

Infantry Brigade in the line had a number of 18-foot trench board pattern foot-bridges for crossing dykes. There were also two Army Pontoon Equipments, and, finally, the bridging equipment of the Field Companies of Divisional R.E.

On the night of October 15th/16th the 1/5th King's Liverpool Regiment forced a passage at Don (where the 423rd Field Company subsequently threw a pontoon bridge), occupied Don, and, on the following morning, the 1/6th King's Liverpool Regiment, crossing the canal on a single plank, drove the enemy from Allenes Annœullin and Chateau Du Bois. During October 16th the 165th Infantry Brigade, meeting with little opposition, occupied Herrin and reached the western outskirts of Gondecourt.

Meanwhile the 164th Infantry Brigade in the Left Section had met with stubborn resistance at the Bac De Wavrin during the 15th and 16th. During the 16th the west bank of the Canal was reached from Les Anscruilles to the Bac De Wavrin, and two light cork bridges were thrown by 422nd Field Company, one across the Haute Deule Canal and one across the Seclin Canal.

In the evening of October 16th, the 165th Infantry Brigade were ordered to advance northward from Herrin so as to facilitate the forcing of the passage at Bac De Wavrin. This was successful, and a pontoon bridge was thrown at this place by the 422nd Field Company.

The Reserve Brigade (166th Infantry Brigade) was ordered forward to the area Grand Rue—Hocron—Marquillies on October 16th, with Headquarters at Petit Moisnil.

Divisional H.Q. moved to Salome on this date.

PHOTOGRAPH OF PORT

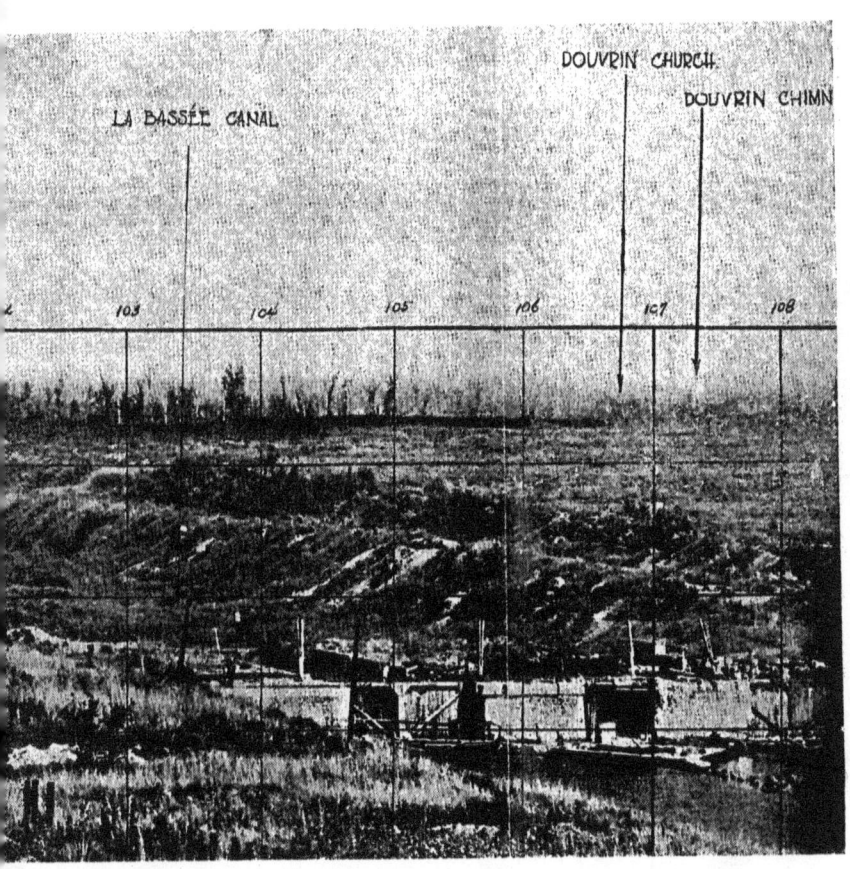

THE GIVENCHY FRONT.

After the crossing of the Haute Deule Canal the advance continued very quickly. On October 17th the 2/5th Lancashire Fusiliers in the Left Section occupied Wattionies and Templemars with little opposition, and found these villages entirely unharmed and still inhabited by the normal civil population. The 1/6th King's Liverpool Regiment in the Right Section occupied Seclin, which was also very little damaged, and the following places were also occupied by 165th Infantry Brigade :— Fort De Seclin, Grand Ennetieres and Fort De Vendeville. At mid-day on October 17th orders were issued for the two leading Brigades to move all their troops to the east side of the Haute Deule Canal as soon as possible. A pontoon bridge was thrown across the Seclin Canal by the 419th Field Company. This bridge was subsequently dismantled and re-erected on October 18th for the use of the Reserve Brigade, which was ordered to Allennes—Gondecourt—Herrin.

Orders were issued for the continuance of the advance on the 18th, in the first instance to the line Grand Ennetieres—Vendeville, and, secondly, to establish an outpost line of resistance on the general line west of Fretin— east of Enchemont. The Reserve Brigade was ordered to Seclin—Templemars.

By the morning of October 18th the first objective had been captured; the enemy, who was met with in small machine gun posts, mostly running away when approached. During the day the advance continued without serious opposition as far as the high ground west of Fretin—Fort D'Enchemont—Enchemont. Beyond this line the opposition was greater; an enemy patrol was dispersed in Fretin, and fighting took place in Peronne, while considerable machine gun fire came from the woods east of La Marcq. By the evening of October 18th our advanced guards had reached the west bank of the Marcq and were in touch with Divisions on each flank. The crossings over the Marcq were mostly secured with bridges prepared for demolition, but intact. At Bouvines the bridge was destroyed, and a 45-foot trestle bridge was thrown, early on October 19th, by the 422nd Field Company, after a crossing had been forced by the 1/4th Royal Lancaster Regiment during the night. It was found that the enemy had withdrawn his machine guns from their positions east of the Marcq. The advance continued with little opposition throughout the 19th October, and by the evening a line approximately north and south through Maraiche was reached, and the following villages had been occupied :—Louvil, Cysoing, Bourghelles, Wannehain, Bachy.

Divisional H.Q. moved to Ancoisne on the 18th, to Enchemont on the 19th and to Cysoing on the 20th.

The outpost line of resistance established by advanced guards on the 19th October was east of Custom House—east of Bois De Moudry—east of Bachy.

Infantry Brigades in the line were ordered to continue the advance from the above line at 10 a.m. on October 20th, by which hour the troops composing these two Brigades were to be closed up so as to be east of a line drawn north and south through the eastern outskirts of Cysoing. The first objective given was east of Froidmont, and thence along the high ground north-west of Froidmont ; the second objective east of Willemeau—Pic-Au-Vent—Reservoir. The Reserve Brigade was ordered to march so as to be at Cysoing by 10 a.m. on 20th October.

In accordance with the above orders the Advanced Guard Battalions (2/5th Lancashire Fusiliers in Left Section and 1/7th King's Liverpool Regiment in Right Section) moved forward at 10 a.m. from the outpost line of resistance. The first opposition met with was from machine guns in Froidmont Village and Chateau. This was overcome by 11-15 a.m., at which time the advanced guard of the right Brigade had gained the whole of their first objective. The advanced guard of the left Brigade met no opposition before reaching the first objective. By 11-40 a.m. the right Brigade had reached the final objective and pushed east of this, establishing a post at the road junction in Ere. The left Brigade secured the final objective, with the exception of the Reservoir, from which considerable machine gun fire was encountered. This represented an advance of over 12 miles in the last four days.

During the night of October 20th/21st the 2/5th Lancashire Fusiliers attacked and captured the Reservoir, taking 24 prisoners.

On October 21st the advance was continued, and considerable machine gun fire was encountered from Longue—Sault Wood, St. Maur, Ere and Faubourgs De Lille, and St. Martin.

By noon Ere had been captured and posts established east of the village, and by 1 p.m. St. Maur was captured and posts established east of it, and in touch with the 16th Division on our right. By the evening our line ran 500 yards east of St. Maur, thence nearly due west, and 500 yards east of Ere—west of Faubourg St. Martin. This brought the Divisional front practically up to the outskirts of Tournai, and here a check was experienced for a considerable time.

On the night 21st/22nd October the 166th Infantry Brigade relieved the 165th Infantry Brigade in the right section, the latter going into Reserve at Bourghelles.

On the morning of October 22nd an attempt was made by 166th Infantry Brigade to seize respectively Barges Chateau and the wood on the high ground west of Faubourg St. Martin. Both attempts were met with very heavy machine gun fire, and were without success. In the evening, under an artillery barrage, the 1/4th Loyal North Lancashire Regiment attacked and captured the wood, but lost it in a hostile counter-attack on the following morning.

During the rapid advance of the last few days a main line of resistance had not been maintained, but Battalions of the leading Brigades which did not form part of the advanced guard were moved forward by Brigadiers as occasion demanded. It was at this date (October 23rd) clear, however, that the enemy intended to hold firmly to the bridgehead which had been established west of Tournai, and which corresponded roughly with the III. Corps front. It was not at this time the Corps policy to attack this bridgehead. It was decided, therefore, during this stationary period, to re-establish a main line of resistance, and, instead of ordering an advance day by day, to give certain areas or objectives for minor enterprises. At the same time systematic and vigorous harassing of the enemy was undertaken daily, both by Artillery, Machine Guns, and Trench Mortars. The main line of resistance selected was west of Froidmont and northward to the eastern slopes of the high ground north-west of Froidmont. The outpost line of resistance was Mont-Au-Gris—Pic-Au-Vent—high ground north of Pic-Au-Vent. A certain amount of artillery was withdrawn to cover the main line of resistance.

Hostile artillery during this period was fairly active, especially on Ere, St. Maur and Willemeau. Froidmont was also shelled with Yellow Cross Gas, and it was found necessary to evacuate the civilians.

On October 25th, at 1 p.m., after a burst of artillery fire, a party of the 2/5th Lancashire Fusiliers captured the Factory between Ere and Barges, taking three prisoners; but the Factory was lost in a subsequent counter-attack.

In order to be ready to follow up and keep touch with the enemy should he retire to a considerable distance east of Tournai, the III. Corps ordered a mobile force to be formed from the Division. The force was put under the command of Brigadier-General C. I. Stockwell, C.M.G., D.S.O., Commanding 164th Infantry Brigade, and its composition was as follows:—

H.Q., 164th Infantry Brigade.	Bourghelles.
" C " Squadron King Edward's Horse.	Cysoing.
" A " Coy. VII. Corps Cyclist Battn.	Cysoing.
" A " Battery 275th Brigade R.F.A.	
2/5th Lancashire Fusiliers.	Bourghelles.
" A " Coy. 55th Battalion M.G.C.	Cysoing.
423rd Field Company R.E.	Cysoing.
(less bridging equipment)	
One Section 2/1st W. Lancs. Fd. Am.	Cysoing.
One Cable Detachment.	Cysoing.
One Wireless Detachment.	Cysoing.
Detachment D.A.C.	Quennaumont.
Detachment Div. Train.	Wannehain.

The various units remained for command and administration under their own Commanders until the force was required to operate. This force was inspected by the Major-General Commanding on October 30th.

During the last few days of the month the hostile artillery was active; and our own artillery carried out daily and systematic bombardments, and, in addition, detached guns or sections did excellent work by driving up into forward positions, opening fire at targets over open sights, and then driving away again.

A certain number of fires and explosions were seen behind the enemy's lines, and information from prisoners and civilians pointed to a contemplated retirement on a large scale; but at this time there was no slackening in the enemy's hold of his bridgehead west of Tournai. It was important to obtain prisoners, in order to discover what were the enemy's intentions at this time. The Brigades in the line were, therefore, instructed to organise raids for this purpose. A raid on the wood west of the Faubourg—St. Martin was arranged for November 2nd, in conjunction with a raid by the 74th Division on our left. The raid was carried out by the 1/7th King's Liverpool Regiment, and was supported by all the Divisional Artillery (except the Advanced Guard Battery of Right Section). The 166th Infantry Brigade in the Right Section also demonstrated with artillery and trench mortars. The raid was preceded by a discharge of harmless gas, which was intended to cause the enemy to put on his gas masks, while it would be unnecessary for the raiders to do the same. The efficacy of this gas was uncertain, but, as far as could be ascertained, the enemy did not put on gas masks. The raid was quite successful; 15 enemy were killed and eight captured.

Heavy machine gun fire was brought to bear on the wood by hostile machine guns from both flanks and the rifle range, and it was evident that the wood was not tenable unless the enemy were also dislodged from the Faubourg west of Tournai. The 74th Division on our left were unable to reach their objective owing to heavy machine gun fire.

The information obtained from these prisoners was that at present no retirement was contemplated, but that they had orders to hold on to their positions at Tournai.

Vigorous artillery and trench mortar harassing fire was carried out daily by the Divisional Artillery, the principal targets being the wood mentioned above, Barges Chateau and the Factory between Ere and Barges. The enemy's artillery was also very active in retaliation, and during all this period the 166th Infantry Brigade were subjected to a constant bombardment of gas and other kind of shell.

On November 5th a well-planned daylight raid by the 1/5th King's Own Royal Lancaster Regiment (166th Infantry Brigade) in the Right Section, was carried out on an enemy post between St. Maur and Barges Chateau. A bombardment was put down at ten minutes to the clock hour, and again at the clock hour, for several hours; and finally at the clock hour, when the garrison of the post was likely to be taking cover, a party went over and captured the post.

Information was received from III. Corps that the withdrawal of the enemy from the Escaut was expected on the night November 5th/6th. Patrols were, therefore, sent out all along the Divisional front, and the following instructions were issued as to the conduct of the advance should such a retirement take place.

(1) The objective of the Corps was Ath.
(2) The first objective of the Division was to establish bridgeheads at Chercq and at the Prison at the south end of Tournai, and make good a line from Gueronde to the Railway just south of Havines.
(3) The second objective of the Division was the high ground west of Barry to the Railway north of Liberchies.
(4) The advance was to be, as before, by advanced guards of Brigades in the line, supported, if necessary, by the remaining Battalions of these Brigades.
(5) Stockwell's force was to be prepared to pass through the advanced guards should opposition cease on the second Divisional objective. The objectives of Stockwell's force were then to be, firstly, high ground west of Leuze; secondly, east of Leuze.
(6) As all bridges over the Escaut were destroyed, bridging material, both light and pontoon, was collected at Esplechin, and placed at the disposal of B.Gs.C. forward Brigades.

Patrols reported at dawn on the 6th that the enemy was still holding his usual positions west of the Escaut.

On the same morning (6th November) three patrols, each of one platoon of 1/5th King's Liverpool Regiment, carried out most successful raids. The right patrol raided the Factory, capturing two prisoners, and, moving along the railway, secured 17 more prisoners in a tunnel under the railway. The centre patrol raided a group of houses north of the Factory, taking one Officer and 34 other ranks, with two machine guns and an automatic rifle. The left patrol was unable to reach its objective. The posts captured were held till mid-day, when the patrols withdrew to their original line.

Information was received from the III. Corps that as the enemy's withdrawal from the Escaut had been so long delayed, it might be necessary to force the passages by an operation on a large scale on the Fifth Army front. A necessary preliminary to this would be the forcing of the enemy bridgehead west of Tournai on the Divisional front, simultaneously with an operation by the Division on our right. The Division was to prepare a plan for occupying the line of the Escaut from Calonne (inclusive) to Chercq, with a flank thrown back to St. Maur. At the same time the 16th Division on our right were to occupy the line of the Escaut from Bruyelle to Calonne (exclusive). Both Divisions were also to form bridgeheads on the east bank of the river.

A plan for this operation was made, and assembly positions chosen. The 166th Infantry Brigade were allotted the task on the right, and the 165th Infantry Brigade that on the left, but on the morning of November 8th it was ascertained that the enemy's posts west of Tournai were withdrawing. Patrols were at once sent out from Brigades in the line, and two prisoners captured stated that the enemy were now holding the east bank of the Escaut. Units of Stockwell's Force were ordered to be at one hour's notice to move. During the morning the advanced guard of 165th Infantry Brigade, in the Left Section (1/6th King's Liverpool Regiment), pushed on, and reached the west bank of the river practically unopposed. Owing to open ground, which was swept by machine gun fire throughout the hours of daylight, the advanced guard of the 166th Infantry Brigade (1/5th South Lancashire Regiment) had some difficulty in clearing the Chercq Quarries, and did not reach the west bank of the river until the afternoon. The same machine gun fire from the east bank prevented any crossing of the river during daylight. One platoon of this Battalion made a particularly gallant effort to save the bridge at Chercq, but came under heavy fire in doing so, losing its Officer and the greater part of the platoon in killed and wounded.

The Infantry of Stockwell's Force was ordered to be concentrated in the Esplechin—Froidmont area in the morning of November 9th.

On the night of November 8th orders were issued to forward Brigades to make every endeavour to cross the river during the night, to follow up vigorously, attack the enemy wherever met; if necessary, using all their Brigades to dislodge him. The remaining two Battalions of 164th Infantry Brigade were placed one each at the disposal of B.Gs.C. forward Brigades.

Stockwell's Force was ordered to be prepared to push through the advanced guard and take up the pursuit at any moment that serious opposition ceased.

During the night 8th/9th November one Company of 1/5th South Lancashire Regiment crossed the river by a footbridge erected by the 422nd Field Company, at Chercq, and two companies, followed later by a third company, of 1/6th King's Liverpool Regiment, crossed by a light bridge erected by the 419th Field Company during the night, just south of Tournai. Both these light bridges were subsequently supplemented by pontoon bridges. Little opposition was encountered, and by

8-30 a.m. on November 9th the whole of the advanced guards of both Brigades were over the river and had reached the line Gueronde—Havinnes, and by 2 p.m. both Brigades were on their second objective east of Barry, in touch with the enemy, who was still retiring.

Stockwell's Force, followed by the 9th Cavalry Brigade (Brigadier-General Legard), which was placed under G.O.C. 55th Division, crossed the Escaut at 3 p.m. Stockwell's Force pushed on towards Leuze, and mounted troops reached the western outskirts of that place at 10-30 p.m. The enemy made a short stand on the high ground east of Pipaix, and on the line Leuze—Gallaix—Maulde. Stockwell's Force established an outpost line for the night 9th/10th November just west of Gallaix, and the 9th Cavalry Brigade billeted about Ramecroix.

Objectives for the 10th November were issued on the evening of November 9th from Chercq, where Advanced Divisional H.Q. was established. Objectives were as follows :—

The 9th Cavalry Brigade (less one Regiment and one Section R.H.A., which was detached to XI. Corps), were embodied in Stockwell's Force, which now came under Command of General Legard. The task allotted to this force was to secure the crossing of the Dendre at Ath.

The first objective of forward Infantry Brigades was a general line just west of Leuze, and the second objective was the high ground west of Chapelle-A-Wattines.

At 8 a.m. on November 10th a message was received from Legard's Force stating that Leuze was clear of the enemy, and that Ligne was only held by small parties.

At 9-25 a.m. the left Brigade reported our Infantry entering Leuze, and both Brigades continuing to push on without opposition, reached their second objectives west of Chapelle-A-Wattines by 1 p.m.

At 11-30 a.m. Legard's Force had cleared Ligne and was moving on Villers St. Amand, and at 12-35 p.m. the advanced troops were checked by hostile machine guns covering the crossings of the Canal at Ath, and the 2/5th Lancashire Fusiliers were moving forward to attack.

By nightfall on 10th November Legard's Force had reached the line of the Blaton Canal and Dendre River, but further advance was checked by machine gun fire, and the infantry attack had not made much progress. The enemy were holding the line of the railway from L'Arbre to Ath, and thence the river west and north of Ath. The mounted troops of Legard's Force were withdrawn for the night, and the 2/5th Lancashire Fusiliers were left as outposts on the line reached, with orders to try and force a crossing during the night or in the early morning.

The advanced troops of the right and left Brigades by dark had reached the line Moulbaix—Villers St. Amand—Willauflosse, the remaining troops of these two Brigades being in and around Leuze. The 1/4th King's Own Royal Lancaster Regiment and the 1/4th Loyal North Lancashire Regiment had moved up during the day from Esplechin, and joined the 166th and 165th Infantry Brigades respectively.

The Division had advanced over 13 miles since crossing the Escaut on the night 8th/9th November, along the main Tournai—Brussels Road, which the enemy had rendered impassable to all but pack transport, by means of craters, inundations and mines. This road was effectually dealt with by the Field Companies and Pioneers, who, in this stretch of road, filled 22 craters; over 500 mines being dealt with by them and the personnel attached from the 170th Tunnelling Company. As a result of this work no delay in getting up transport was experienced, even lorries being able to move along the road the day on which the Escaut was first crossed; a crib and rail bridge to take 17 tons being erected where the road crossed the River Dendre by the 422nd Field Company.

On the night November 10th orders were issued giving a general plan for the attack on Ath for November 11th, should the crossings of the Canal and River not have been forced during the night. The 165th and 166th Infantry Brigades were to attack immediately south and north of the town respectively, the 2/5th Lancashire Fusiliers were to hold the enemy frontally, and the mounted troops were to make a turning movement as far north as circumstances permitted.

A conference for all Commanders was ordered for 9 a.m., November 11th, at Headquarters, Legard's Force, at Villers St. Amand, to settle details of plan, by which time all troops taking part in the attack were ordered to be in preliminary assembly positions.

No crossing of the bridges into Ath was effected during the night 10th/11th November. Two bridges remained intact, namely, that on the main Leuze—Ath Road just north of Ath, and the iron bridge on the Irchonwelz—Ath road just south of Ath.

At 5-30 a.m. on November 11th the Lancashire Fusiliers reported that the iron bridge was barricaded and mined, and still held by the enemy. By 7 a.m., however, by means of daring action, during which a Lewis gun was mounted in a house close to the bridge, the enemy was driven from the bridge without being able to blow it up, and the barricade was destroyed. The Lancashire Fusiliers passed into the town, and the mounted troops pushed on ahead, reaching the line Ponchau—Renard by 8 a.m. The Lancashire Fusiliers reached the same line shortly afterwards, and the mounted troops pushed on with little opposition eastward. At 9-5 a.m. a verbal message was received at Divisional Headquarters, which was at Barry, and was telephoned from there to the Conference which was taking place at Villers St. Amand, stating that hostilities would cease at 11 a.m., and troops would at that hour stand fast on the most easterly ground held.

Orders were issued to this effect, but did not reach the advanced mounted troops until 1-30 p.m., by which time they were on the line Thoricourt—Bassilly, over seven miles east of Ath.

The 166th and 165th Infantry Brigades were ordered to take up an outpost line on the high ground Brugelette—Mevergnies—Ghislenghien, passing through the 2/5th Lancashire Fusiliers, who were on the line Ponchau—Renard. The remainder of 166th and 165th Infantry Brigades were ordered to be concentrated in billets behind the outpost line. The Lancashire Fusiliers were ordered to withdraw as soon as the outpost line was established to billets at Villers St. Amand, where the 1/4th King's Own Royal Lancaster Regiment and the 1/4th Loyal North Lancashire Regiment were to rejoin. Divisional Artillery was ordered to billets in Douaire and Antoing. The mounted troops were to be withdrawn at dusk and billeted at Ligne, less 9th Cavalry Brigade, which ceased to be under the Division. The Machine Gun Battalion, other than Companies with

Outposts, were to billet at Andrecourt and But, and the Field Companies and Pioneers were ordered to billet along the main road between Leuze and Ath. Divisional Headquarters was established at Chapelle-a-Wattines.

The furthest point reached by the Division was the line Bassilly—Thoricourt, which represents an advance from the Givenchy—Festubert line of over 50 miles in 80 days.

CHAPTER VII.

THE LAST PHASE.

Here, then, at Ath the fighting history of the Division ends. The rest was but a period of waiting for Demobilisation. The Division had been selected to proceed to the Rhine to form part of the Army of Occupation, and the march tables for the purpose were in course of preparation. The orders were, however, subsequently cancelled and, instead, on December 14th the Division proceeded by road to Brussels, and Divisional Headquarters opened at the Chateau Errera, near the Bois de la Cambre, on the 16th. The units were quartered in the suburbs of Uccle, St. Job, Watermæl, Forest, Ruysbrœk, and Linkebeek, all within easy distance of the city, and the attractions of Brussels and its neighbourhood provided a very welcome variation of the daily routine. Lectures, educational courses, football matches, cross-country runs, boxing competitions and the like passed the time pleasantly, and occasional visits to the neighbouring battlefield of Waterloo suggested illuminating comparison between the methods of war a hundred years ago and the methods of to-day.

On January 3rd—the 3rd anniversary of its formation in France—the Division had the honour of being reviewed in the Bois de la Cambre by H.M. the King of the Belgians, who warmly expressed his appreciation of its soldierly appearance. Lord Derby—who had come up from Paris to visit the Division—was present at the Review, and afterwards renewed his old acquaintance with many of the units. On this day, every Officer,

Non-commissioned Officer and man in the Division received a copy of the following, which was very much appreciated :—

"55TH (WEST LANCASHIRE) DIVISION.
"SPECIAL ORDER OF THE DAY.
"In the Field,
"3rd January, 1919.
"Soldiers of the 55th Division.

"To-day is the third anniversary of the formation of your Division in France. With the exception of short periods of rest, amounting to about four months in all, the Division has been in active daily touch with the enemy throughout these last three years, until the conclusion of the Armistice. During the whole of that time it has been my great privilege to command it. So to-day I want to give a message to every soldier, of all ranks, now with the Division, and, through them, to everyone of the sixty thousand who have served in it, and are still living.

"Many, I am glad to say, who saw the formation of the Division are with us now, but very many more, who were serving then in the Division, or who have served since, are not. There are some still suffering from wounds, and some whose graves we have left on hard-fought fields and behind grim trench lines, where they faced the enemy with such splendid courage and determination. They are not forgotten.

"The Battles of the Somme, Ypres, Cambrai and Givenchy—Festubert took heavy toll of the Division, and the long, wearisome trench warfare was not less costly. But every battle, and all the days of trench fighting, showed more and more clearly as time went on the stuff of which the Division was made, and enabled it to establish and maintain the proud reputation which now belongs to it.

"We have gone through hard and anxious times together. Yet, however dim and far off ultimate victory seemed, you never faltered or lost heart; you showed the same stubbornness in defence as you have shown boldness in attack. There was a time when things seemed almost desperate; when we were forced by weight of numbers to await, day after day, fierce attack by a confident and relentless enemy. You knew how things were; knew that, as the Field-Marshal Commanding-in-Chief said in his Order of the Day, you stood with your backs to the wall; but this knowledge only added to your dogged determination—and you won through. The glorious victory you gained in the fighting from the 9th to the 16th April, 1918, when, outnumbered and with your flank turned, you withstood for days, without yielding ground, a series of violent attacks by an enemy already flushed with success; and, taking advantage of every opportunity for the offensive, inflicted on him the severest losses, was the first bright spot after many dark days. You may fairly claim to have left on him a mark that he carried to the end, and to have done your full share towards his ultimate destruction. It is believed that the front held by the Division was the only piece of the Allied front, which, being attacked in force during the German offensive of 1918, was held to the end inviolate.

"All commanders and staffs, all arms and services, and all ranks, have played their part equally loyally. I want to thank you all for what you have done, to tell you how highly I value the support and trust you have always given me, and how intensely proud I am to have commanded such a Division in such a war.

"What has stood us in the greatest stead throughout has been the magnificent spirit of comradeship that has run all through the Division, so that everyone has played up, not for himself, but with complete unselfishness for the good of the side, and with complete trust in his comrades. Such comradeship is the foundation and essence of true discipline.

"Another great asset has been the unfailing cheerfulness with which dangers and hardships have been faced. I have never found a man of the Division who had not a smile ready, even in the blackest times.

"Courage, determination, endurance, cheerfulness, unselfishness, these are the virtues that have pulled you through, and brought us victory at last.

"Peace, we believe, will now soon be firmly established, and then we shall all be scattered. But, wherever we go, I hope we shall all still feel that we belong to the 55th Division, and shall still retain the spirit that has made it what it is. You all know of the 55th Division Comrades' Association which has been formed. Its object is to keep up in peace the spirit of comradeship which has bound us together in face of the enemy, and to enable us to stand by each other in the future as we have in the past. I hope you will all join it.

"As, owing to the manner in which demobilisation is to be carried out, I may not have another opportunity, I wish everyone now in the Division—or who has been in it—success and happiness in whatever he may undertake.

"H. S. JEUDWINE, Major-General,
"Commanding 55th (West Lancashire) Division."

Very soon after this the Division began to melt away; slowly at first, then with increasing rapidity. Presently the 55th Division will be but a name, and a proud memory. But in the years to come the thoughts of those who fought in its ranks will many a time hark back, with pleasant reminiscence, to the days of stress and endurance; to the life-long friendships begotten, strengthened and sustained during those years of fiery trial; and to those one-time comrades who paid with their lives the price of the triumph they themselves were never to see.

The old spirit of comradeship is not to be lost, however. Very soon after the cessation of hostilities a desire was spontaneously expressed that the links which had bound together all ranks so splendidly during the fighting days, and had made of the Division not merely a first-class fighting unit but a happy family, should not rudely and suddenly be severed. Delegates, therefore, from every unit in the Division assembled in the Theatre at Ath on December 2nd, under the presidency of the Major-General, and with enthusiasm it was there and then determined to form a Comrades' Association, in which all who had fought in the ranks of the Division were to combine to perpetuate this spirit of comradeship, to promote and to safeguard each other's interests, to perpetuate the memory of the fallen and to promote the welfare of their dependants, and to arrange for frequent re-unions of the members.

And it was decided that the Red Rose, which we had worn so proudly on our shoulders in war, should be the badge of our mutual recognition in the days of peace.

APPENDIX I.

THE DISTINGUISHING BADGES OF THE DIVISION.

On the 30th March, 1916, an order was issued directing that distinguishing badges of coloured material were to be worn by all ranks just below the collar at the back of the S.D. jacket.

The badges worn by Battalions are shown below.

164th INFANTRY BRIGADE.

1/4th King's Own R. Lancs. Regt.   1/8th King's Liverpool Regt.

2/5th Lancs. Fusiliers.   1/4th Loyal N. Lancs. Regt.

165th INFANTRY BRIGADE.

1/5th King's Liverpool Regt.   1/6th King's Liverpool Regt.

1/7th King's Liverpool Regt.   1/9th King's Liverpool Regt.

166th INFANTRY BRIGADE.

1/5th King's Own R. Lancs. Regt.

1/10th Liverpool Regt. (Scottish)

1/5th South Lancs. Regt.

1/5th Loyal N. Lancs. Regt.

ROYAL ENGINEERS.   ROYAL ARTILLERY.

419 Field Company R.E.

[275 Bde. R.F.A.

422 Field Company R.E.

276 Bde. R.F.A.

423 Field Company R.E.

Divl. Ammn. Column

Pioneer Battalion 1/4th South Lancs. Regt.

APPENDIX II.

Numbers of all ranks who have passed through the Division between Jan. 3rd, 1916, and Nov. 11th, 1918.

Officers	2,870
Other ranks	61,053
Total	63,923

Battle Casualties.

	Killed.	Wounded.	Missing.	Total.
Officers	385	1,028	168	1,581
Other ranks	6,135	23,266	4,719	34,120
Totals	6,520	24,294	4,887	35,701

Percentage of casualties all ranks	55%
Average daily casualties (1,044 days)	32

List of Honours gained by the Division, Jan. 3rd, 1916—Nov. 11th, 1918.

Bar to the Victoria Cross	1
The Victoria Cross	11
K.C.B.	1
C.B.	3
C.M.G.	8
O.B.E.	2
Bar to the D.S.O.	12
D.S.O.	68
Second Bar to the M.C.	3
Bar to the M.C.	64
M.C.	360
O.B.E., Class 4	1
Bar to the D.C.M.	3
D.C.M.	197
Second Bar to the Military Medal	1
Bar to the M.M.	76
M.M.	1,572

Meritorious Service Medal	70
French Honours and Decorations	23
Belgian	40
Italian	7
Russian	5

To give the citations of all the acts of gallantry for which honours have been awarded would take more space than is available. A list of the citations upon which the Victoria Cross has been awarded is, however, herewith appended.

2nd Lieut. (T. Lieut.) E. F. Baxter, 1/8th Liverpool R. (T.F.), V.C.

For most conspicuous bravery. Prior to a raid on the hostile line, he was engaged during two nights in cutting wire close to the enemy's trenches. The enemy could be heard on the other side of the parapet. 2nd Lieut. Baxter, while assisting in the wire cutting, held a bomb in his hand with the pin withdrawn, ready to throw. On one occasion the bomb slipped and fell to the ground, but he instantly picked it up, unscrewed the base plug and took out the detonator, which he smothered in the ground, thereby preventing the alarm being given, and undoubtedly saving many casualties. Later, he led the left storming party with the greatest gallantry, and was the first man into the trench, shooting the sentry with his revolver. He then assisted to bomb dug-outs, and finally climbed out of the trench and assisted the last man over the parapet. After this he was not seen again, though search parties went out at once to look for him. There seems no doubt that he lost his life in his great devotion to duty.

3153, Rifleman A. Proctor, 1/5th Liverpool R. (T.F.), V.C.

Opposite Ficheux, after an attempted raid on the German trenches had taken place at midnight on 3/4th June, 1916, it was thought that all the wounded men had been brought into our lines before daylight. Apparently, however, two men who were lying between the German trenches and our own had lost consciousness after being wounded, and about midday on the 4th June, movement was noticed on the part of these men. The distance from the British Front Line to them was about

75 yards—for the most part in full view of the enemy. Proctor, entirely on his own initiative (for no order could be given as the journey seemed certain death), ran and crept out until he reached the side of the wounded men, being frequently fired at during this time. Under shelter of a slight bank where they lay he dressed their wounds, cheered them up generally by his visit and promise of speedy assistance at dusk, divested himself of his jersey and put it on one of the men suffering from the cold, and then in the same manner as mentioned above, regained our lines. As a result probably of this act of gallantry he had the satisfaction later of seeing the two wounded men brought back alive to our lines at night.

2579, Pte. James Hutchinson, 2/5th Lancashire Fusiliers (T.F.) V.C.

For great gallantry and bravery when engaged in a raid on the German trenches opposite Ficheux on June 28th, 1916. He bayonetted and shot at least eight Germans and single-handed held the enemy at bay, covering the retirement of his party until they had withdrawn from the trench. It was largely due to his gallantry and initiative that the party was able to withdraw and bring back the wounded men to our trenches.

2nd Lieut. Gabriel George Coury, 3rd S. Lan. R., attached 1/4th S. Lan. R. (Pioneers), V.C.

For signal gallantry and devotion to duty, initiative, coolness, and the highest qualities of leadership displayed on the morning of 8th August, 1916, between Arrow Head Copse and the German Front Line, when in command of two platoons of the 1/4th S. Lan. R. (Pioneers). The attack was delivered at 4-20 a.m. 2nd Lieut. Coury took his two platoons out at 4-22 a.m. to dig a communication trench from the old firing line to the new position gained by the attacking troops. During the progress of the work, 2nd Lieut. Coury patrolled the line of the trench under heavy fire, and by his coolness and utter disregard of personal safety, kept the spirits and confidence of his men until the task was successfully completed.

Owing to the loss of most of the Officers, the attacking troops commenced to retire. Lt.-Col. Swainson, 1/4th R. Lanc. R. went out to restore confidence, and ordered his men to dig themselves in at the end of the communication trench dug by the Pioneers.

Shortly afterwards, 2nd Lieut. Coury, hearing that Lt.-Col. Swainson had been hit, immediately, in broad daylight, and in full view of the enemy, went out in front of the advanced position to find him and, having found him, brought him in over ground traversed by machine gun fire, to the new advanced trench, being met and assisted by Pte. Haworth of the 1/4th R. Lanc. R. A sergeant of the 2/2nd West Lancs. Field Co., R.E., had previously been killed in rendering assistance to Lt.-Col. Swainson. 2nd Lieut. Coury not only successfully carried out the task assigned to his detachment, but assisted in rallying the attacking troops and leading them forward.

Capt. Noel Godfrey Chavasse, R.A.M.C. (T.F.), attached 1/10th Liverpool R. (T.F.), V.C.

For exceptional bravery and devotion to duty.

During the attack on Guillemont on August 9th this Officer continued to tend the wounded in the open all day under a heavy fire, frequently exposing himself to view of the enemy. He organised parties to get the wounded away most successfully. That night he spent four hours searching the ground in front of the enemy's lines for wounded lying out. On the following day he proceeded with one stretcher bearer to the advanced trenches, and carried an urgent case for 500 yards to safety under a very heavy shell fire. During this performance he was wounded in the side by a shell splinter. The same night he took up a party of 20 volunteers, and succeeded in recovering three more of the wounded from a shell hole 25 yards from the German trench, buried the bodies of two Officers, and collected a number of identity discs, although fired on by bombs and machine guns. Altogether this Officer was the means of saving the lives of 20 seriously wounded men under the most trying circumstances, besides the ordinary cases which passed through his hands. At one time, when all the Officers were shot down, he helped to rally the firing line.

200717, Cpl. (L/Sgt.) Thomas Mayson, 1/4th "King's Own" R.L.R., V.C.

For most conspicuous gallantry, daring and devotion to duty during the operations on 31st July, 1917, near Wieltje.

During the advance the leading wave, of which this N.C.O.'s platoon formed a part, was held up by machine gun fire from a flank. L/Sgt. Mason, without waiting for orders, immediately made towards the machine gun, taking what cover he could. He succeeded in bombing the gun, putting it out of action and wounding four of the team. The remainder of the team, three in number, bolted to a dug-out, into which they were pursued by L/Sgt. Mason, and killed. If it had not been for this N.C.O.'s immediate and daring action, the leading wave would have been checked, and would have lost its barrage and perhaps failed to make progress.

Later on, when mopping up an enemy strong point, his platoon was again exposed to the fire of another machine gun. L/Sgt. Mason again tackled the gun and team single-handed, knocking out the gun and killing six of the team.

Later, during an enemy counter-attack, he took charge of an isolated post with one Lewis gun and four men, and successfully held up the advance at that point until all his ammunition was exhausted.

Capt. Noel Godfrey Chavasse, V.C. M.C., R.A.M.C. (T.F.), attached 1/10th Liverpool R. (T.F.), Bar to V.C.

For most conspicuous gallantry and undaunted devotion to duty in action in front of Wieltje between July 31st and August 2nd, 1917.

Early in the action he was severely wounded in the head whilst carrying a wounded man to his dressing station.

He refused to leave his post, and not only for two days continued to attend to the cases brought to his regimental aid post, but repeatedly, under heavy fire, went out to the firing line with stretcher parties to search for wounded and dress those lying out.

During these searches he found a number of badly wounded men in the open, and assisted to carry them in over heavy and difficult ground. He was practically without food during this period, worn with fatigue, and faint as the result of his wound.

By his extraordinary energy and inspiring example he was instrumental in succouring many men who must have otherwise have succumbed under the bad weather conditions.

On the morning of August 2nd he was again wounded seriously by a shell, and died in hospital on August 4th.

This most gallant Officer was awarded the Military Cross for gallantry in action at Hooge on June 16th, 1915, and he received the Victoria Cross for conspicuous bravery in the rescue of wounded under fire in action at Guillemont on August 9th, 1916.

Capt. (A/Lt.-Col.) Bertram Best-Dunkley, 2/5th Lancashire Fusiliers (T.F.), V.C.

For very conspicuous gallantry, soldierly ability and devotion to duty when in command of the battalion at Wieltje on 31st July, 1917.

The leading waves, advancing to the attack, suddenly came under heavy rifle and machine gun fire at close range from positions which were believed to be in our hands. This threw the front of the attack into confusion.

Lt.-Col. Best-Dunkley dashed forward, rallied his leading waves, and personally led them to the assault of these positions, which, despite heavy losses, were carried. He continued to lead his battalion until all their objectives had been gained.

Had it not been for this Officer's gallant and soldierly action, it is doubtful if the left of the brigade would have reached its objectives.

Later in the day when our consolidated line was threatened, he collected his battalion headquarters and led them to the attack, and beat off the advancing enemy. He continued to hold this position till he was wounded, from the effects of which he has since died.

681886, Sgt. Cyril Edward Gourley, D/276 Battery, R.F.A. (T.F.), V.C.

For very conspicuous and continuous gallantry and devotion to duty while fighting his section of 4.5in. Howitzers on 30th November, 1917, near Little Priel Farm, East of Epehy.

When the enemy advanced in force against the left of the 55th Divisional front, the Officer in command of the section was wounded at once, and Sergeant Gourley was sent forward to ascertain the situation, no Officer being available.

He found that the enemy was 400 yards in front of the guns, between 300 and 400 yards to one flank, and snipers in the rear. In spite of this he managed to keep one gun in action, and manned it from 10-30 a.m. till dark.

All day the gun was a direct target to the enemy from three sides, and was continually under fire from artillery, aircraft, infantry, machine guns and snipers.

Sergeant Gourley was frequently driven off by artillery and machine gun fire, but always returned and re-opened fire, carrying ammunition, laying and firing the gun himself, taking first one and then another of the detachment to assist him.

When the enemy advanced down Holts Bank in full view, Sergeant Gourley pulled his gun out of the pit into the open, switched it round, and engaged in a duel with a machine gun at 500 yards which the enemy had set up in Holts Bank.

This machine gun was in rear of our posts firing into the back of our infantry, and at the gun. He knocked it out with a direct hit, and stopped the enemy advancing.

All day he held the enemy in check, firing with open sights on enemy parties which were in full view at 300 to 800 yards. He engaged any target that appeared, in spite of the continued hostile artillery, machine gun, and rifle fire.

His tenacity and coolness under fire in fighting his gun prevented any further enemy advance at this point. This would have entailed the loss of the guns, which were successfully withdrawn at nightfall.

Awarded the Military Medal for conspicuous gallantry at Ypres in July, 1917.

2nd Lieut. Joseph Henry Collin, 1/4th R. Lanc. R. (T.F.), V.C.

For most conspicuous gallantry, devotion and self-sacrifice in the action at Givenchy on 8th April, 1918.

After offering a long and gallant resistance against heavy odds in the Keep held by his platoon, this Officer, with 5 only of his men remaining, slowly withdrew in the face of superior numbers, contesting every inch of the ground. The enemy were pressing him hard with bombs and machine gun fire from close range. Single-handed 2nd Lieut. Collin attacked the machine gun and team. After firing his revolver into the enemy, he seized a Mills Grenade and threw it into the hostile team, putting the gun out of action, killing 4 of the team, and wounding two others.

Observing a second hostile machine gun firing in front, he took a Lewis gun, and selecting a high point of vantage on the parapet whence he could engage the gun, unaided he kept the enemy at bay with fire until he fell mortally wounded. His heroic self-sacrifice was a magnificent example to all.

2nd Lieut. John Schofield, Lancashire Fusiliers, attached 2/5th Lancashire Fusiliers (T.F.), V.C.

For most conspicuous bravery and devotion to duty in operations against the enemy at Givenchy on the 9th April, 1918.

He led a party of 9 men to a strong point, which was reported strongly held by the enemy.

A party of the enemy about 100 strong attacked his party with bombs. 2nd Lieut. Schofield disposed his men so skilfully, and brought such rifle and Lewis gun fire to bear, that the enemy took cover in dug-outs. This Officer himself then held up and captured a party of twenty.

With the help of other parties, this position was then cleared of the enemy, who were all killed or captured. He then collected the remainder of his men, made his party up to ten, and proceeded towards the front line, previously sending back a message to his Commanding Officer as to the position, and that he was proceeding to take the front line. He met large numbers of the enemy in a communication trench in front of him, and in a drain on right and left. His party opened rapid rifle fire, and he climbed out on to the parapet at point blank machine gunfire, and by his fearless demeanour and bravery forced the enemy to surrender.

123 of the enemy, including several officers, thus surrendered to 2nd Lieut. Schofield and his party.

A few moments later he was killed.

15883, Lce./Cpl. James Hewitson, 1/4th R. Lancs. R. (T.F.), V.C.

For conspicuous gallantry, initiative and daring in action near Givenchy on the 28th April, 1918.

In a daylight raid on a series of crater posts, this N.C.O. led his party to their objective with dash and vigour, clearing the enemy from both trench and dug-outs. In one dug-out he killed six of the enemy who would not surrender. On the capture of the final objective he observed a hostile machine gun team coming into action against his men. Working his way round the edge of the crater, he attacked the team. Five of them he killed outright; the sixth surrendered. Shortly after he engaged a hostile bombing party, which was attacking a Lewis Gun point. He routed the party, killing six of them.

These extraordinary feats of daring crushed the hostile opposition at this point.

APPENDIX III.

The First Operation Order Issued by the Division.

Reference map
Lens sheet 1/100,000.   9th February, 1916.

1. The 55th Division will relieve the 88th French Territorial Division holding the line from R.31.d.4.1 to R.23.d.10.5.

2. On the 12th and 13th February the 166th Infantry Brigade 2/1st West Lancashire Field Company and 2/1st West Lancashire Field Ambulance will relieve that portion of the French line known as the Riviere Sector, now held by the 176th Infantry Brigade (French) with Headquarters at Basseux.

3. The 165th Infantry Brigade, one Company Pioneers (1/4th South Lancashire Regt.) and 2/1st Wessex Field Ambulance will take over the Wailly Sector from 176th Infantry Brigade (French) with Headquarters at Beaumetz, as follows:—

  (a) On the night 14/15th February, two Battalions of the 165th Infantry Brigade will relieve the 82nd Regiment holding the Ficheux Sub-sector.

  (b) On night 15/16th February, headquarters, two battalions and one company Pioneers (1/4th South Lancashire Regiment) will complete the relief of the Left Sector, relieving the 81st Regiment holding the Marboueuf Sub-sector.

4. The lines of demarkation of Areas, &c., and dispositions of Troops are shown on map "A" issued herewith to Brigades, B.G.C.R.A., and C.R.E.

5. The necessary moves and reliefs will be carried out in accordance with the attached march table.

6. The details of relief will be arranged between Brigades concerned.

7. The Reliefs of the Artillery will be arranged by the B.G.C., R.A., of the Division in consultation with the Commandant of the 88th Division Artillery.

The Artillery will commence reliefs on night 15/16th February, one Section of each battery relieving a corresponding section of a French Battery that night. The remaining section will complete the relief on the night 17/18th February.

8. Movements on the roads East of a line drawn through Beaumetz, Basseux, Berles-Auxbois will not take place by day in larger bodies than Platoons of Infantry, or similar numbers of other formations, at 200 yards intervals. Due precautions will be taken against observation by hostile aeroplanes.

9. Divisional Headquarters will close at Domart at 6 a.m. on the 16th February and re-open at Gouy at the same hour, when the Major-General Commanding the Division will take over Command of the line now held by the 88th Territorial (French) Division.

J. K. COCHRANE, Lieut.-Colonel,
Issued at 8 a.m.   General Staff, 55th (W. Lancs.) Division.

The Last Operation Order Issued by the Division.

Senders number G.C. 18.   Day of month 10th.

Operation Order. Enemy has to-day been pressed back East of Canal at Ath where he now holds the crossings. If the crossing of the Canal is not effected during the night, it is intended to attack enemy to-morrow with Legard's Force 165th and 166th Infantry Brigade and attached troops. Legard's Force less mounted troops will engage enemy from West of Ath. 165th and 166th Infantry Brigades will be prepared to make encircling attacks N. and S. of Ath respectively. Mounted troops of Legard's Force will be withdrawn to position of assembly from which they will be prepared to make a Northern turning movement as wide as circumstances permit. C.R.A. will arrange for Divisional Artillery other than that of Legard's Force to support the attack, and for 1st West Riding Heavy Battery to be disposed so as to be able to shell the Ath Brussels Road East of Ath.

Details of Operation will be settled to-morrow at Conference to be held by Divisional Commander at H.Q., Legard's Force N.9.d.9.4 at 0900 by which hour troops will be assembled in following preliminary positions: Guji with attached M.G. Co. about N.8.a., 275th Brigade R.F.A. about M.6.d. and M.2.b., Gule and attached M.G. Co. about M.26.b. and d., 276th Brigade R.F.A. about N.25.c. and 31.a. Artillery Brigade Commanders will arrange with B.G.'sC. of Infantry Brigade to which affiliated, so that march of Artillery to these assembly places does not delay march of Infantry. Following will attend Conference mentioned above:—C.R.A., B.G.'sC., Buna, Guji, Gule and Legard's Force, O.C., 275th and 276th Brigades R.F.A., O.C., 1st West Riding Heavy Battery, O.C., M.G. Battalion B.

Acknowledge. (Signed) R. T. LEE, Lieut.-Col.,
From Yee timed 2100 hours. G.S., 55th Division.

The Conference was held at 9 a.m. on 11th November as arranged. During the Conference, at 9-30 a.m., a telephonic message was received from IIIrd Corps stating that the armistice had been signed and that Operations would cease at 11 a.m.

The following telegram was thereupon sent to all Units:—
G.B. 40—11

Reference cessation of hostilities movement of troops will be as follows and will be carried out with all military precautions. AAA Stockwell's Force is on line Ponchau Renard 1.33.Cent with K.E.H. forward of this. 165th and 166th and their attached troops will move through Stockwell's Force and establish outpost line as follows O.24. O.18. P.1. J.31. J.26 dividing line between Brigades crossing of stream in P.1.c. Remaining troops of 165th 166th will be concentrated in rear of outpost line. 166th Brigade will move from present position via bridges at N.12.c.5.2. and O.7.c.1.1. Brigade Headquarters at Ponchau. 165th Brigade will move via main Leuze Ath Road and cross river by bridge at N.6.c.6.5. if intact. Pontoon equipment has already been placed at disposal 165th Brigade Headquarters to O.4.a. As soon as Outpost line established Stockwell's Force less mounted men will be withdrawn to billetting area between Villers St. Amand and W. of Ath where 1/4th King's Own

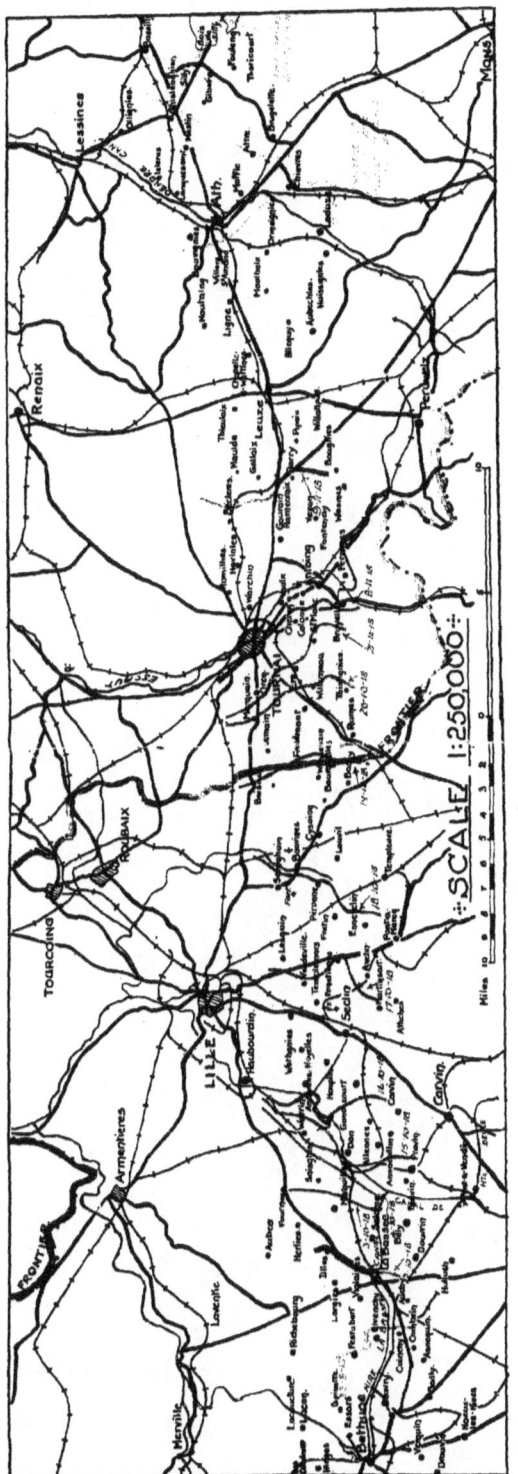

Map shewing the Advance October 2nd to November 11th, 1918.

and 1/4th L.N. (Lancs. and T.M.B. will rejoin. Div. Arty. less Adv. Guard batteries will move to billets in Antoing and Douaire. Heavy Artillery to Gromont. Mounted troops Stockwell's Force will be withdrawn at dusk and billet at Brewery in Ligne. M.G. Bn. less Coys. with Adv. Guards will move to billets at Andricourt and But. Field Coys. and Pioneers as far as their work permits will billet near main road in N.9.d. Separate orders will be issued for move of D.A.C. Headquarters, 164, Villers St. Amand., Div.: H.Q. Chapelle-a-Wattines. Troops not to enter Ath or Leuze without passes which should be sparingly given and for stated hours.

Acknowledge.   (Signed) R. T. LEE, Lieut. Col.,
Time, 1115.   G.S., 55th Division.

APPENDIX IV.

WORK OF R.E. AND PIONEERS DURING THE ADVANCE, FROM AUGUST TO NOVEMBER, 1918.

From August to 2nd October.

Bridges.

Trestle Bridges, 60 feet span, for Light Transport ...	2
Trestle Bridges, 60 feet span, for Lorries	1

From 3rd October (Capture of La Bassee) to 7th November.

Bridges.

Pontoon and Trestle Bridges, 60—70 feet span	10
Floating Foot-Bridges, 70 feet span	4
Brick Arch Bridges strengthened to take 17 ton Axle Loads	3

(Timber for this work was felled on the site).

Roads.

Horse Transport.

Miles.

Entirely new road	¾
Total length of portions of roads actually made good ...	8¼

Heavy Transport.

Total length of portions of roads actually made good ...	5¼
Road widened from 10 to 18 feet	¾

Craters.

Large road craters filled and made good for heavy transport, including 10 over 60 feet diameter and 15 feet deep	32

From 8th November (Capture of Tournai) to 11th November (Armistice).

Bridges.

Pontoon and Trestle Bridges, 105 feet span	2
Floating Foot-bridges, 105 feet span	2
Heavy Rails and Crib Piers, 18 feet span, to take 17 tons Axle Load	2

Roads.
Heavy Transport.   Miles.
Total length of portions of roads actually worked on ... 14

Craters.
Large road craters made passable by lorries 22

Mines.
Total number removed, more than 500

SUMMARY.
Bridges.
Floating Foot-bridges 6
Pontoon or Trestle 14
Trestle, &c., for Heavy Traffic 3
Arch Bridges strengthened 3

Roads.
Horse Transport.   Miles.
New ... ... ¾
Made Good 8¼

Heavy Transport.   Miles.
Widened ... ... ¾
Made Good 19½

Craters.
Filled 54

During the period 8th-11th November, a careful record was kept of the distance marched and hours worked by the R.E. and Pioneers. These average as follows:—

    Marched ... ... 9¼ Miles per day.
    Actual working hours in addition
        to the March ... ... 9 Hours per day.

BATTLE CASUALTIES

Incurred by Units, Jan. 3rd, 1916—Nov. 11th, 1918.

		Killed or Died.	Wounded.	Missing.
Divisional Headquarters.				
	Officers	1	1	—
	Other ranks	3	5	—
		4	6	—
Royal Artillery.				
Headquarters	Officers	—	1	—
	Other ranks	—	2	—
275th Brigade, R.F.A.	Officers	7	29	1
	Other ranks	76	438	38
276th Brigade, R.F.A.	Officers	5	27	—
	Other ranks	111	456	1
277th Brigade, R.F.A.	Officers	3	5	—
	Other ranks	16	55	—
Divisional Ammunition Column	Officers	—	2	—
	Other ranks	21	92	—
Div. Trench Mortar Batteries	Officers	3	6	2
	Other ranks	30	175	28
		272	1,286	70
Royal Engineers.				
419 Field Company	Officers	—	8	—
	Other ranks	28	147	16
422 Field Company	Officers	6	9	—
	Other ranks	66	141	9
423 Field Company	Officers	4	12	—
	Other ranks	46	303	28
Div. Signal Company	Officers	1	3	—
	Other ranks	9	58	1
		160	681	54
164th Infantry Brigade.				
1/4th King's Own Royal Lancaster Regiment	Officers	38	107	10
	Other ranks	469	1,955	392
2/5th Lancashire Fusiliers	Officers	58	120	8
	Other ranks	800	2,500	360
*1/8th (Irish) King's (Liverpool Regt.)	Officers	25	75	10
	Other ranks	450	1,500	400
1/4th Loyal North Lancs. Regt.	Officers	31	79	13
	Other ranks	386	2,099	310
		2,257	8,435	1,503

		Killed or Died.	Wounded.	Missing.
165th Infantry Brigade.				
1/5th King's (Liverpool Regiment)	Officers	20	61	18
	Other ranks	370	1,731	446
1/6th King's (Liverpool Regt.)	Officers	26	69	11
	Other ranks	564	1,871	194
1/7th King's (Liverpool Regt.)	Officers	19	64	6
	Other ranks	402	1,486	223
1/9th King's (Liverpool Regt.)	Officers	22	22	3
	Other ranks	249	752	52
		1,672	6,056	953
166th Infantry Brigade.				
1/5th K.O. Royal Lancaster Regt.)	Officers	20	66	20
	Other ranks	383	1,114	408
1/10th Liverpool Scottish	Officers	20	61	20
	Other ranks	433	1,603	567
1/5th South Lancashire Regt.	Officers	16	63	24
	Other ranks	441	1,373	606
1/5th Loyal North Lancs.	Officers	30	28	13
	Other ranks	408	1,333	473
		1,751	5,641	2,131
1/4th South Lancashire Regt. (Pioneer Battalion)	Officers	12	55	1
	Other ranks	160	1,245	45
		172	1,300	46
55th Bn. Machine Gun Corps.	Officers	10	42	4
	Other ranks	153	623	102
		163	665	106
Divisional Train, R.A.S.C.	Officers	—	1	—
	Other ranks	11	27	—
		11	28	—

		Killed or Died.	Wounded.	Missing.
Royal Army Medical Corps.				
1/3rd W. Lancs. F. Ambulance	Officers	1	2	1
	Other ranks	18	45	14
2/1st W. Lancs. F. Ambulance	Officers	1	3	—
	Other ranks	9	41	—
2/1st Wessex F. Ambulance	Officers	2	2	—
	Other ranks	17	73	5
		48	166	20
Royal Army Chaplains Department.				
	Chaplains	4	4	2
Mobile Veterinary Section.				
	Officers	—	—	—
	Other ranks	1	5	—
Military Police and Traffic.				
	Officers	—	1	1
	Other ranks	4	10	—
D.A.D.O.S.				
	Officers	—	1	—
	Other ranks	1	—	—
246th Employment Company.				
	Other ranks	—	9	1
Totals	Officers	385	1,028	168
	Other ranks	6,135	23,266	4,719
		6,520	24,294	4,887

* No return from this unit being available, approximate numbers are given.

APPENDIX I.

THE DISTINGUISHING BADGES OF THE DIVISION.

On the 30th March, 1916, an order was issued directing that distinguishing badges of coloured material were to be worn by all ranks just below the collar at the back of the S.D. jacket.

The badges worn by Battalions are shown below.

164th INFANTRY BRIGADE.

1/4th King's Own R. Lancs. Regt.   1/8th King's Liverpool Regt.

2/5th Lancs. Fusiliers.   1/4th Loyal N. Lancs. Regt.

165th INFANTRY BRIGADE.

1/5th King's Liverpool Regt.   1/6th King's Liverpool Regt.

1/7th King's Liverpool Regt.   1/9th King's Liverpool Regt.

166th INFANTRY BRIGADE.

1/5th King's Own R. Lancs. Regt.

1/10th Liverpool Regt. (Scottish)

1/5th South Lancs. Regt.

1/5th Loyal N. Lancs. Regt.

ROYAL ENGINEERS.   ROYAL ARTILLERY.

419 Field Company R.E.

[275 Bde. R.F.A.

422 Field Company R.E.

276 Bde. R.F.A.

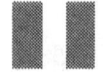

423 Field Company R.E.

Divl. Ammn. Column

Pioneer Battalion 1/4th South Lancs. Regt.

www.ingramcontent.com/pod-product-compliance
Lightning Source LLC
Chambersburg PA
CBHW031253230426
43670CB00005B/169